Ryuho Okawa, founder and spiritual leader of the Institute for Research in Human Happiness (IRH), has devoted his life to the exploration of the spirit world and ways to happiness.

He was born in 1956 in Tokushima, Japan. After graduating from the University of Tokyo, he joined a major Tokyo-based trading house and studied international finance at the City University of New York. In 1986 he renounced his business career and established IRH.

He has been designing IRH spiritual workshops for people from all walks of life, from teenagers to business executives. He is known for his wisdom, compassion and commitment to educating people to think and act in spiritual and religious ways. The members of IRH follow the path he teaches, ministering to people who need help by spreading his teachings.

He is the author of many books and periodicals, including *The Laws of the Sun*, *The Golden Laws*, *The Laws of Eternity*, and *The Starting Point of Happiness*. He has also produced successful feature length films (including animations) based on his works.

For further information on The Institute for Research in Human Happiness (IRH) please contact: tokyo@irh-intl.com.

By the same author

The Laws of the Sun
The Golden Laws
The Laws of Eternity
The Starting Point of Happiness
Love, Nurture and Forgive

The Essence of
BUDDHA

The Path to Enlightenment

RYUHO OKAWA

timewarner
paperbacks

A *Time Warner* Paperback

First published in Great Britain in 2002 by Time Warner Books
Published by Time Warner Paperbacks in 2003

Translated by The Institute for Research in Human Happiness Ltd.
Original title: *Shaka-no-Honshin*

A CIP catalogue record for this book
is available from the British Library.

ISBN 0 7515 3355 6

Typeset by M Rules
Printed and bound in Great Britain
by Clays Ltd, St Ives plc

Time Warner Paperbacks
An imprint of
Time Warner Books UK
Brettenham House
Lancaster Place
London WC2E 7EN

www.TimeWarnerBooks.co.uk

Contents

CHAPTER THREE

The Six Paramitas

CHAPTER FOUR

The Idea of the Void

Contents

Preface to the First Japanese Edition

It gives me great pleasure to publish this book, *The Essence of Buddha*. The first chapter tells the story of how Shakyamuni renounced the secular life and attained the great enlightenment; then, in the following chapters, I have explained in a modern and systematic way the very essence of the laws he taught. I intend to offer a complete account of Shakyamuni's life at some other time, but in the meantime in this volume I have presented an overview of his thought. I trust that you will find a clear picture of the basic framework of Shakyamuni Buddha's thought. The main ideas such as the Noble Eightfold Path, the Six Paramitas, the Void and the Law of Causality are explained in such a way that it will be easy even for a reader who has little previous knowledge of Buddhism to understand.

I hope that this book – which, like *The Laws of the Sun*, *The Golden Laws* and *The Laws of Eternity*, came into being through spiritual revelation – will nourish the hearts and minds of many.

Ryuho Okawa, August 1988

CHAPTER ONE

The Enlightenment Under the Bodhi Tree

The Renunciation of a Secular Life

In this book, I would like to explore what was really in the mind of Gautama Siddhartha, who later became known as Shakyamuni Buddha or simply the Buddha, to focus on his enlightenment and what he did after. For this reason, rather than giving extensive background information, I will attempt to describe how Gautama attained enlightenment after he renounced his secular life as a prince, how he lived out his long years of teaching the Truth to the public, with emphasis on what he thought during that period from the point of view of his innermost self. Much Buddhist literature has already described his renunciation of the secular life, and I would say that the contents of those texts are mostly correct.

There were three main reasons why Gautama renounced the secular life. The first was an inner voice that urged him to do this. He heard it say that in life at the royal palace he could not fulfil his yearning, and that something greater, something unknown was awaiting him. If I attempt to explain his feelings in the context of modern society, he could be likened to an ambitious youth who leaves his rural hometown to achieve something big and distinguish himself in the world. Rather, it might be more accurate to attribute this inner prompting to his innate nature, or foreknowledge of his calling.

The second reason is often described in various Buddhist traditions as Gautama's search for an answer to the questions of the Four Pains, the pains of birth, of aging, of illness, and of death. A well-known allegory goes like this: 'There were four gates at the Kapilavastu palace. When he went out of the east gate, he met an old man who looked haggard. Going out of the south gate he met someone suffering from illness, at the west gate, he saw someone who was sick and dying, and at the north gate he met an ascetic who had renounced the secular life.' According to legend, it was only after encountering those four people that he began to wonder why people suffer the Four Pains of birth, aging, illness and death. However, it would have been practically impossible for him not to have been aware of human suffering until the age of twenty-nine. In actual fact, the real reason for his renunciation was different.

The palace of Kapilavastu, which was Gautama's home, had a custom of inviting men of religion to give lectures once a month. Just as it is the custom of the present Japanese Imperial Family to invite scholars to deliver lectures, so too the Royal Palace in ancient India one day invited a man who had attained a certain level of enlightenment to come and speak, so that they could learn from him.

Together with other members of the royal family, Gautama would listen to the talks of those religious teachers. Although the people around him were deeply impressed, he was unable to find answers to his inner questions. He had a strong philosophical urge to know what it was that those people were actually pursuing, what enlightenment really was. The second reason for his renunciation of the secular life was an inner prompting to search for answers to the questions he had about the words of the religious masters who had been invited to the palace.

The third reason was his strong desire to be alone, to remain absorbed in contemplation. Gautama had a highly meditative nature; from early teenage years, he was fond of contemplating in solitude. However, the social customs of that time required that the prince marry, and formal wedding ceremonies were held for him. He actually had four wives: in order of social status, Yashodhara was the most exalted, then came Gopa, followed by Manodhara, and a beautiful concubine, Murgaja, who had been a lady-in-waiting.

The reasons for the custom of polygamy in the royal family at that time can be explained as follows: 1) to increase the chances of securing a royal heir; 2) to provide a choice of more than one palace as a domicile, each with a wife, to lessen the risk of an enemy attack on the king (prince); 3) to reduce the risk of the overbearing influence of one particular wife on the government of the state; 4) to demonstrate royal dignity.

Gautama first took the beautiful Gopa as a wife, then he married the exalted and aristocratic Yashodhara as his 'first lady'. She later withdrew from the world to become a nun, following the path of her son Rahula, Gautama's only heir who had become a monk.

Talking with his wives, Gautama could not help wondering why women were unromantic and liked to gossip so much. He became very tired of the jealousy and possessiveness they exhibited. In this sort of environment, it was extremely difficult for him to practise meditation or enjoy philosophical contemplation. Gradually, he developed a craving to be alone.

To be fair to the four wives of Gautama, however, I would like to add that they were all clever and beautiful women, suitable wives for a future king. If Gautama were to succeed his father to the throne and govern the country, as was expected, there would have been no problem. The truth is that there was no woman who could match his philosophical genius.

Apart from these ladies, Gautama was also surrounded by many court attendants, both men and women. Every single decision he made required their acknowledgement, and every time he moved, he had to be accompanied by people-in-waiting. He wanted to escape this sort of life and just reflect on himself, alone.

Moreover, the social custom of the day in India allowed those who had provided an heir to carry on the family line and sufficient wealth to support their wives and children to renounce the secular life and go into the forests or mountains as ascetics. To put this custom into a modern context, it would be like leaving your home town to pursue your ambitions in a big city, or like going abroad to study.

Seeking a Teacher

After leaving the royal palace at the age of twenty-nine, Gautama began wandering the country looking for someone to guide him. His search for a teacher and his undertaking of ascetic discipline have been described in various Buddhist texts.

His journey in search of a teacher and all the austerities he went through were not in vain; to some extent they contributed to his spiritual growth. For one thing, he had the chance to observe the life of seekers and what they were seeking. What he discovered can be summarized under two main points.

Firstly, in India at that time, the worship of superhuman abilities was common, and people had a strong yearning to go beyond this world. Many people wanted to find some means or other to escape the afflictions of this world and to become superhuman. Secondly, he observed a general trend of pursuing methods of achieving true happiness. In other words, people were pursuing the principles of happiness so many teachers were competing in the art of explaining how human beings could achieve happiness.

One teacher taught that torturing the body was the shortest way to enlightenment, and that the less physical one became, the closer one came to enlightenment. Based on this belief, people walked on fire, sat cross-legged underwater in meditation, stood on their heads, cut and pierced their own bodies with blades and needles, and so on.

Another teacher concentrated on stopping thought. He reasoned that the source of life's difficulties was the thoughts that pass through the human mind. If people could only stop thinking, all worries would disappear and people could enjoy the supreme joy of tranquillity. This could be described as the origin of the modern idea of 'meditation to think nothing'.

Yet another teacher pursued what would now be called debating skills, without clearly defining what enlightenment was. His studies focused on how to elude verbal assaults, and his idea of enlightenment seemed to be winning arguments.

Through contact with these people, Gautama started to feel that there was something wrong with the attitude of those seekers. Everything they were teaching seemed pointless. He found that no matter how hard he tried to look for answers, no one could give him a clear description of what the purpose of life was, or the truth about the spirituality of human beings. He stopped searching for a teacher less than a year after he renounced the secular life. Then, taking his own heart and mind as his teacher, he began seeking a way to find the Buddha in himself. In this way, discovering the laws of Truth became the purpose of his self-discipline.

Ascetic Trainings

Having abandoned the search for a teacher, Gautama quietly entered the forest by himself. Attaining enlightenment on his own became his objective, and he tried every possible way of training he could think of, until he finally discovered his own method.

He spent some time deep in thought, in forests infested by poisonous snakes. At dawn, he would be meditating on the side of the Nairanjana River. He would sometimes spend all night wide-awake, unable to sleep, or in broad daylight he would just sit still, perspiring. Looking at leaves in the jungle, sitting in meditation in a cave, or looking at the surface of a river, he was silently and constantly looking for a way of attaining enlightenment.

Gautama's search for a teacher lasted less than a year. The conclusion he reached, as a result of his training with two famous hermits – Alara-Kalama, who taught meditation in the state of nothingness, and Udraka-Ramaputra who taught meditation in a state where neither thought nor no-thought existed — was that concentration was important above all else. He had mastered the ways of attaining peace of mind through meditation, but the fruits he obtained from this discipline could be described as just mental states; he could not find a Truth that could be explained logically. The reason he left those two teachers was that he wanted to attain wisdom, rather than to meditate just for the sake of meditation.

The initial objective of his austerities was to get rid of any concern for worldly matters. For this reason, he chose to live in the remotest places away from all villages. He tried to eliminate his worldly desires, but the first difficulty he experienced was food, as the lack of it exacerbated his desire to get something to eat at any cost. The truth he discovered at that time was that although human beings have various sorts of desires, when one particular desire grows disproportionately large, the others become less distinct. When he had not eaten anything for days, he found that his desire to eat grew so intense that the desire for sleep and sexual desire gradually faded, but they never completely disappeared. Living on berries, leaves and other edible things he could find in the woods, Gautama's physical strength naturally declined, and his legs gradually became weaker. Eventually, he could find only enough strength to sit in meditation in the cave.

Self-Reflection

Several years passed, and Gautama would spend most of his days in his cave, except for a few hours when he would go out to get something to eat, for sustenance. During that period, Gautama contemplated deeply on the following questions: For what reason were human beings born? Why do they come into this world that is afflicted by incessant war? Would the path to becoming an 'awakened one' that so many people talked of really lead to the other shore, to happiness? Although many people abandoned their secular lives, and avoided facing the difficulties of a life spent in constant struggle, what became of them? Did they attain enlightenment? Did they enter a world of true tranquillity after leaving this world, detached from the world of pain? Nobody has ever been able to confirm that. Were they simply deluding themselves, unable to confirm they were on the right track?'

He also reflected deeply on himself. 'Several years have already elapsed since I left Kapilavastu. I wonder how my father, King Shuddhodana, my step-mother Mahaprajapati and the people-in-waiting are faring? How upset my wife Yashodhara will be! How is my only son Rahula doing? I have renounced my worldly duties, broken away from family ties in pursuit of enlightenment, but will I ever attain enlightenment? Have I even got any closer to enlightenment, or have I become a better person? Have I understood the purpose or the mission of life?'

However, no matter how hard he tried to abandon his worldly desires, his attachment to them only intensified. The harder he tried to forget all his relationships with others, the more concerned he became about them. As he continued to listen to the sound of the water dripping from the ceiling of the limestone grotto he was sitting in, reduced to skin and bones, he could not help reflecting deeply on whether the path he was following was really the right path for enlightenment.

As the days passed, he could hardly contain the thoughts pressing on his mind, about how much longer he could carry on by himself and hold to his firm resolve. He even started to wonder whether it was time to go back to the royal palace that had been his home. As he tried to fend off these thoughts, he often found himself almost losing consciousness.

5

A Village Girl

Gautama then left his cave at Gayasisa (or Elephant Head
Peak) near Gaya, the capital of the ancient kingdom of
Magadha, and walked on towards the River Nairanjana. In
the Uruvilva-Senani village beside the river, he entered a
new phase of his discipline. The village, now known as
Sujata, is a very scenic place; there was always a refreshing
breeze and it was an ideal setting for his practices of self-
discipline. There were beautiful forests and a clear stream
with such an abundance of water that it sometimes nearly
carried Gautama's thin body away when he was bathing.

One day, he noticed a village girl singing on the other side
of the river. Her voice somehow reminded him of the
human world close to his heart, while at the same time, it
sounded like music from heaven. The song was a traditional
Indian folksong, about a musical instrument similar to a lute.

The song went, '. . . the strings of the lute snap when they
are tightened too far. When they are too loose, the sound
becomes dull. They sound good when they are moderately

14

tight. Dance and dance to the sound of strings. Let's dance and dance to the sound of strings . . .'

Listening to the girl singing, Gautama was struck by how different he must look in comparison with her. To his eyes, she looked just like an angel, with flaxen hair, her eyes shining brilliantly, her body filled with vitality, and her whole presence radiating a lovely fragrance, almost out of keeping with her humble standing as a mere village girl. In contrast, Gautama's body was reduced to skin and bone, he looked just like a skeleton. His eyes were sunken and his ribs were protruding. It looked as if his life was about to end at the age of thirty-five.

When she caught sight of Gautama, she came running across the bridge towards him, introduced herself as Sujata, and offered him a bowl of milk porridge. The moment he tasted the porridge, warm tears trickled down his cheeks. Although it was not in any way a luxurious dish, the milk porridge tasted almost heavenly to Gautama, who had been surviving on berries and the roots of grasses. It could be said that he shed tears of shame at his own state, feeling the emptiness of being completely immersed in ascetic discipline, and having abandoned joy in life.

He said to himself, 'If, through this sort of self-discipline, I am only reduced to skin and bone, and ultimately risk cutting my life short, how much beauty does that hold? How much value could there be in that? Probably this girl, Sujata, has never even thought about enlightenment. She may never have studied any religious doctrine, or undergone any spiritual discipline, but why is she shining so brilliantly, as if she were from heaven?' The difference could be explained as the difference between one who was going to go on living and another who was about to come to the end of his life. When tears welled up unwittingly and wet his cheeks, he was surprised that he still had tears to shed. He became aware of feelings of misery and loneliness that filled his heart, as one who was about to abandon life and intended to die. This encounter with the village girl gave Gautama a clue about the next step. He was going to turn thirty-six in a few months.

The Will to Live

The encounter with Sujata gave Gautama the strong message that he needed to build himself up. The tears that washed down his cheeks might have been a farewell to his past. When the milk porridge reached his stomach, imparting a sense of strength and richness, he became aware that the denial of food did not necessarily lead to Truth. He thought that, from the perspective of the food itself, it may be a joy to be eaten by people and be used for a higher plane of human activity, because in this way it was not wasted.

He thought, 'Everything in this world must exist as material to serve something more exalted. Judging material things to be meaningless because they are this-worldly is probably merely arrogance on the part of a seeker of Truth. Of course, if materials are left as they are, they may not produce any results, but it may be a good idea to think of worldly matter as ingredients for cooking. If the Divine is watching us, He would be pleased to see us making these ingredients into splendid dishes.'

In this way, Gautama firmly resolved to change his life; it was as if he had been born again. The tears that streamed down his cheeks, the warmth and strength of the food that filled his stomach and the radiant, vital energy of Sujata, all of these helped him to embark on a new stage in his search. On top of these, one phrase of Sujata's song powerfully inspired him.

The phrase 'The lute sounds good when the strings are moderately tight' brought to Gautama's mind a well-known truth that if strings are tightened too far they may snap, but if they are too loose, the sound that comes out is not right. He thought, 'Now, I am probably like a string that has been tightened to its absolute maximum that the slightest touch would snap. This state can never produce truly good music. I have been undergoing extremely rigorous discipline to attain enlightenment, but this sort of life is not worth as much as that of a girl who lives quite naturally. If the door to the heaven were to open now, and it was a choice between Sujata and myself, there is no doubt it would open for her, not for me, who looks like someone out of hell. If only I am allowed to live a little longer, even just a few more years, I would like to restore my body and find the true meaning of life in this world, not just a negative understanding but also the positive meaning.'

The very moment when this enthusiasm to live welled up within may have marked Gautama's first step on the path to enlightenment in a truest sense. He could not help but doubt that he could attain enlightenment through ascetic discipline alone. If he had continued with such extreme austerities, he thought, he would simply have died, and if human beings were only born to die, then human life in this world would be completely meaningless.

Pressing his hands together and bowing to Sujata to express his gratitude, Gautama bid her farewell and set out on his way. As he looked around, everywhere he saw signs of life. The grasses, the flowers, the trees were all full of life but he found that he had been so preoccupied with his discipline that he had neglected to observe the vigor of nature all around him.

'The tiny flower at the roadside adds beauty to nature, so if it only wanted to wither and eventually disappear, this world would be a little less beautiful. What if all the animals were weary of living, and wanted to die as quickly as possible? What if the cows or the horses only wanted to lose weight, and refused to eat? What if they refused to bear offspring?' Thoughts like these flashed through his mind.

Peace of Mind

At that point, Gautama decided to accept offerings of food. He usually stayed at this chosen spot, in the grove of Uruvilva. Twice a day, early in the morning and again in the afternoon, he made regular rounds to the villagers' houses to gather alms, and accepted with gratitude the food that people respectfully offered him.

Soon after he decided to accept these offerings, he found peace and harmony were developing within him. He had been too concerned about being independent, whether it was in collecting food or getting other necessities, and had refused to accept any help from others. Realizing that he was constantly in a state of extreme tension, just like strings of a lute that have been tightened too much, he reminded himself of the importance of moderation. In his actual position, as a devout seeker of Truth, he was, of course, not capable of satisfying his everyday needs himself. He decided to accept his situation as it was and ask for alms, without putting any undue strain upon himself, and abandoning all pretence, instead of lying to himself that he did not really have an appetite.

In India it was commonly believed that supporting seekers who had abandoned their secular lives was one way of storing up treasure in heaven. So, for pious people of those times, giving offerings was a ceremonial custom and, at the same time, a discipline of accumulating virtue as a lay practitioner of religious faith. Against this background, Gautama decided to accept the offerings happily. Except for the time he spent in gathering alms, he dedicated himself wholeheartedly to deepening his thoughts, to attain enlightenment.

As his excessive concern with independence and his extreme tension disappeared, Gautama realized that a certain relaxation was showing on his face; he could smile again. As his body, which had been reduced to skin and bone, regained flesh, he felt energy and vitality fill him. He realized how feeble he had been, overcome by passive and negative thoughts. He was surprised, as he became more relaxed about life, how precisely he was able to observe others.

He thought he wanted to look at people's lives, and to be able to give each person advice that was appropriate, also to assess himself accurately. He wanted to understand the meaning of this world and human life, and actually experience the enlightenment that so many seekers search for. He really wanted to know what it meant to be a Buddha or an enlightened one, and to understand the state of a Buddha.

Gautama felt he heard a voice saying, 'Give up your old life and take a new path,' so he set out on his way. As he had decided to accept alms from people, it did not matter where he lived. Previously, he had chosen to live where there were berries or edible grass roots, but now that he was living on people's offerings, he did not need to be concerned about such matters. He wished to observe the world and be in touch with the minds of as many people as possible, to deepen his thought. With this intention, he set out on a journey. Several days later, he arrived in a town called Gaya.

The Battle Against Evil in the Mind

Gaya was a town of quite considerable size with fairly busy shopping streets and a population of several thousand. It was in this town Gautama took up the life of a mendicant. During the day, he did his rounds gathering alms, and from dusk to dawn he set aside time for his quest for enlightenment. He made it a rule to start meditating at sunset, under a big pipal tree (also known as an asvattha) not far from the river. As the tree was so vast that two people could not encircle its trunk with their arms outstretched, it provided him with ample shelter.

He concentrated mainly on reflective meditation. Simply trying to focus his mind on a single thought with his eyes closed tended to invite the intervention of evil spirits, so in order to achieve harmony of mind, he focused on reflecting upon what he had thought and what he had done since he was a small child. If he found situations where he had gone against his conscience, he tried to put them right.

However, as the reflection proceeded and he reached the years of his late twenties, Gautama found it impossible to find a solution to a particular thought that overwhelmed his mind, no matter how hard he tried to clear it. It was the thought of his wife Yashodhara and his son Rahula. Their faces haunted him and made him wonder how big his son had grown, how his wife was doing, and whether she was crying over his absence. It unsettled him badly.

By that time, a window in Gautama's mind had started to open onto the spiritual path, and he could hear the voices of beings from the spirit world. When he was sitting in meditation under the pipal tree, a voice began speaking to him from within his mind.

'Gautama, I am Brahma, and I am speaking to you. You have spent six years in austerities, in search of enlightenment, but look at what you have achieved as a result of your hard work. It seems that you have simply proved you are an ordinary person. You have neglected the basic requirements of being human, which are to get married, raise a family and live happily with your wife and children. But look at yourself. You have abandoned your family and the happiness you could have derived from it for the sole purpose of sitting in meditation under a pipal tree. Your life is completely meaningless. You are wrong. Return to the palace of Kapilavastu at once and make your wife and child happy. Living happily with them will pave the path to a great enlightenment for you.

'A human being can never experience happiness in the next life without having enjoyed this one to the full. Take as much pleasure as you like in this world. Enjoy this world as fully as you wish. The greater your joy, the more happiness you will experience in your next life. Are you really enjoying life enough? Enjoy your family life to a greater extent. Feast on a more affluent and elegant lifestyle. That is how you should carry out your self-discipline in this life.'

Gautama found some truth in what the person who introduced himself as Brahma said. It was not only reasonable and convincing, but the remark even touched a soft spot. He was feeling regret at abandoning his wife, and he still felt a strong attachment to his father, his step-mother and other people who had raised him lovingly. The fact that he was not a good son, a good husband, or a good father, could not be undone, no matter how hard he tried to repent. His mind was swayed and he wondered whether he really should return home to the Kapilavastu palace and succeed his father to the throne.

However, the last remark the self-proclaimed Brahma made caught his attention: 'The more you enjoy this world, the more pleasure you will have in your next life.' It sounded plausible, but Gautama felt that something was slightly wrong with the logic, although it was carefully glossed over.

It occurred to him that his attachment to this world, which was still deep in him, might have been brought out, and that the being that called itself Brahma must be a devil. Gautama found out its true identity, and cried, 'You must be a devil. You call yourself Brahma, but you are most definitely not. Admit that you are really a devil, who deludes many seekers. You are Mara Papiyas the devil; you cannot deceive my eyes.' The moment Gautama said this, the voice changed to high-pitched laughter, 'Ha-ha-ha! Well done, Gautama, you've found out. How advanced you are in your training! Good luck with your asceticism, and live a futile life!'

This incident reminded Gautama powerfully that the devil was actually within his own mind. It was not really the devil that troubled him, but the truth was that the weakness or obsession that existed within him had attracted an evil spirit. Unless he rid himself of these attachments, there was no way he could attain a calm state of mind. Even natural, humane thoughts about his wife and son, or his father and mother, when they persisted and were transformed into obsessive attachment, would cause him to suffer. Through that soft spot the devil had made its way into his mind.

Consequently, ridding himself of attachments became the main objective of Gautama's self-discipline. That experience gave him a clue and led him to think deeply about getting rid of attachments in the world of the mind, which was different from giving up the desire to eat, or being satisfied with humble food and clothing.

9

The Great Enlightenment

As a result of his confrontation with the devil named Mara Papiyas, Gautama understood that any worldly desire could be an invitation to devils. In the innermost core of a person's mind, in the recesses of the subconscious, are guardian spirits and guiding spirits, but evil also lurks there. The evil is attracted to the dark thoughts that lie hidden in a person's mind and it feeds on them. Whenever it can find the chance to catch a person off-guard, it has the ambition of taking total control of a person's mind and manipulating them.

In his reflective meditation, Gautama continued to reach more and more refined states. He learned that no matter what kind of thoughts he had, when his mind stopped to focus on a single thought, and clung to it, that would eventually cause suffering. He understood, 'The mind should always be free of attachment, like a mountain stream that flows freely, without restriction. If the mind concentrates on any one thought, whether it be good or bad, the freedom of the mind is lost. As a result, the stagnant spot becomes an easy target for evil, but this situation should not be left as it is. I had better abandon any sense of obligation and instead enter a state of mind that is freer, more open, richer, and more peaceful.'

When Gautama completed his reflection on his whole life of nearly thirty-six years, discarding any negative thoughts that obsessed his mind, and became free of attachment, a great sense of peace enveloped him. It was a completely different sensation from the time before when Mara had appeared. He felt the warmth of heavenly light flowing into his chest, and it was at that moment Gautama heard the voice of Brahma.

'Gautama, we are glad that you have at last attained enlightenment. We have been watching over you, and for a long time we have been waiting for you to reach this first level of enlightenment. Without this enlightenment, you could not fulfil your mission in this lifetime. We were so concerned when you became immersed in a life of luxury and worldly pleasure. We were also worried right after you started your austerities that you might die from malnutrition or commit suicide. However, you have overcome the difficulties and reached this stage, where you are able to hear our voices. We are truly delighted.'

The voice was actually that of Gautama's brother souls who had incarnated on Earth in the past, Rient Arl Croud, Hermes and others. They appeared under the name 'Brahma', conforming to the beliefs of India at that time.

With the ability to see through past, present and future, Gautama then penetrated the secrets of the origin of the universe, the birth and history of the planet Earth, the rise and fall of civilizations, his own past incarnations and the future history of humanity. When his mind became still and free from attachment, he experienced his spiritual body expanding to become as big as the whole of the universe, leaving his physical body behind beneath the pipal tree. This experience distinguishes one who has unlocked the door to the kingdom of the mind, and it is proof of one who has fully grasped the feeling of the perfect freedom of the soul through the spiritual senses. I may have another opportunity to talk about this experience of Gautama's in greater detail, but in summary I can say that Gautama's realization that the soul and the physical body are different marked the very first step for his great enlightenment.

The First Great Step Forward

So Gautama attained his initial enlightenment under the pipal tree (the tree that became known as the Bodhi tree, meaning 'the tree of enlightenment'). Having experienced the highest level of enlightenment, it is natural to want to remain at the level that has been attained, but people tend to become lost in ordinary, everyday life. Gautama was no exception.

Having attained enlightenment and become what we now know as the Buddha, Gautama thought he could not wait to convey what he had understood to as many people as he could, as quickly as possible. He felt that if he kept the experience to himself, his life would have been meaningless, so when he went begging, he did not simply receive alms but tried to take every opportunity to tell the people he met that he had become enlightened, and to share his experiences with them. But nobody would listen. People said that he must have gone crazy, and that he was conceited, because they thought that enlightenment could not be attained unless one studied under a teacher.

His desire to convey that exhilarating experience of enlightenment to others was so intense that he set out to look for the five ascetics he knew from before and talk to them. They were studying with the hermit Udraka-Ramaputra, and when they witnessed that Gautama had reached the same level of enlightenment as their teacher in such a short time, they decided to leave their teacher and go through ascetic training with Gautama.

That was how his teaching of the Law started, but first came his desire to convey what he had become aware of through his enlightenment. Starting from this desire to convey what he had experienced to those who were following the same path to enlightenment, he took the first step forward. Thinking to himself, 'This should be the very beginning of conveying Truth, this should be the initial turning of the Wheel of the Dharma,' his heart beat fast and he felt a strength flowing into his veins. Between the desire to convey Truth to others and another desire to reach a deeper level of enlightenment, he felt he could not sit still, for even a day.

CHAPTER TWO

The Discovery of the Noble Eightfold Path

What is the Noble Eightfold Path?

In this chapter, I would like to talk about the Noble Eightfold Path, one of the best-known teachings of Shakyamuni. When he attained enlightenment under the Bodhi tree, he had already had the concept that would later develop into the Noble Eightfold Path but he had not reached the stage of creating a methodology from it. It was another year before he was ready to teach the idea in the form that is known today.

For a year after he attained his enlightenment through meditation, the Buddha deepened his thought through conversations with close disciples and other people he met. He began to feel that in order to convey the enlightenment he attained, he needed to develop an expedient method that would appeal to the hearts of people. He also became aware of the need to teach the Truth in a way that was different from that of many religious teachers of those times.

As a result of deep and careful contemplation, Shakyamuni Buddha reached the conclusion that his teachings should centre on an objective, attaining a 'right' state of mind. How can we achieve a right state of mind? To attune our mind to a right state, we need to examine our state of mind as compared with a more placid state, closer to that of Buddha (God). Shakyamuni called this state Buddha-nature or the True Self.

As we live our everyday lives and come into constant contact with others, we tend to be swayed by an incessant flow of thoughts, and it is difficult to know the True Self that lies deep within us. However, when we retreat from everyday contact, away from others and from their vibrations, and reflect deeply on our own mind, we can find the True Self. When people are around, we may try to put on an act, maybe out of vanity or to offset our feelings of inferiority, but when we sit alone in meditation, the part of us that is true and honest will emerge. This is the purest part of our soul, connected to Buddha. The very beginning of the Noble Eightfold Path is to examine our own thoughts and deeds from the perspective of this True Self.

Shakyamuni Buddha established eight checkpoints against which people can examine their own thoughts and deeds: Right View, Right Thought, Right Speech, Right Action, Right Livelihood, Right Effort, Right Mindfulness and Right Concentration. He put the adjective 'right' to the eight directions of the mind and the actions of the physical body: seeing, thinking, speaking, acting, living, making diligent efforts, the use of the will, and meditating. 'Rightness' in the Noble Eightfold Path does not imply a simple set of

model behaviours against which people can judge themselves to be right or wrong; it means a 'right' state that can
only be attained through deep contemplation.

Shakyamuni usually practised self-reflection in the
evenings or at the break of day. As he continued to examine
his own thoughts and deeds, spending about twenty minutes
on each of these eight checkpoints, he experienced his mind
gradually becoming lighter and being purified.

2

The Mysteries of
Self-Reflection

Having outlined the Noble Eightfold Path as a method
of self-reflection, I would now like to explain why it
is necessary to practise self-reflection. In fact, self-reflection
is the method through which you can recover your authentic self that shines, your True Self in the Real World. You
may be aware that beyond this world on Earth, there is a
multi-layered structure that consists of the fourth, fifth,
sixth, seventh, eighth and ninth dimensions, and it is in the
seventh dimension and above that the human soul shines
with genuine, brilliant light. Actually, the method of self-
reflection that Shakyamuni taught can be described as a
method of reaching the state of the seventh-dimensional
Bodhisattva Realm.

The first step you need to take to reach the state of
Bodhisattva is to remove the dust or the impurities that overshadow your soul, to return to a state in which you give out

bright light. Only after you have reached the stage where your inner light is shining forth can you really help others. To benefit others by giving out what you have attained is the mission of Bodhisattva, but before that it is necessary to take command of your own inner world.

Let me explain this idea with examples from everyday life. Suppose you want to wipe some dishes. If the dishcloth is dirty, no matter how carefully you try to clean a plate with it, your effort will be wasted. The first thing you have to do is clean the dishcloth. In the same way, if you want to wipe the floor, you will want to use a clean mop. Suppose you want to dress up. No matter how beautifully you are dressed, if you have dirty underwear on that you have not changed for many days, people will not be impressed. Or, consider the teacher who does not have sufficient learning; no matter how hard he tries to teach his students, it is unlikely that they will really improve.

What I have attempted to explain through these examples is that while it is quite easy to have altruistic thoughts, you cannot truly benefit others or help them, unless you are firmly established in yourself. For this reason, it is essential to have taken the first step of 'cleaning' your own soul, so that your inner light can shine forth. This is one of the great secrets of self-reflection.

Each and every human being is given complete autonomy over their own state of mind. Before you can achieve any concrete results in helping others to allow their inner light to shine, it is absolutely essential that you have experienced the feeling of lightheartedness as unnecessary burdens are lifted;

then a bright light will shine forth from within. Only after this has occurred can you teach others what self-reflection is.

There is a danger that if this idea is interpreted in a narrow way it may be misunderstood and seen as egotistical, but unless you are ready to improve yourself, you cannot even take your place at the starting line to study the Laws of Truth. Those who are not willing to control themselves and constantly improve themselves are not qualified to study the Law. For such people, the Law has no meaning or value; it is like the biblical phrase, 'casting pearls before swine'.

Right View

Now, I would like to explore the meaning of Right View, the first path of the Noble Eightfold Path. To put it simply, seeing rightly means seeing the world without any bias, being free of all prejudice, but with deep spiritual wisdom. It seems that most human sufferings originate with the act of seeing. It could be said that if you could not see, you would be less prone to commit sins, because desire is often magnified by the information that comes through the eyes, for example, desires connected to other people, particularly members of the opposite sex, to money, to expensive jewellery and to gourmet dishes.

It is important to know how to sort out the visual data that comes to you every day, because it often stirs human emotion. To be able to sort through this, it is necessary to reflect calmly on yourself at the end of a day, breathing deeply and regularly, to find harmony within. When you have reached a state where you can feel one with Buddha and a powerful light is flowing into you through the golden channel that connects you to heaven, you should examine objectively what you saw during the day, looking at yourself as if looking at a total stranger.

'Seeing' in Right View eventually comes down to decisions about how to perceive what you have seen. Each person has a different view of the actions of others. Let me give you an example that you may come across at work. Suppose a new recruit has made a proposal about a general management strategy for the entire company. How people view this action will vary from person to person.

If you were in the position of this young man's supervisor, you might view him either positively or negatively. If you tended to see things positively, you might think of him as high-spirited, forward-looking and full of promise. On the other hand, if you tended to see things negatively, you might think it is too soon for the young man to talk of a grand plan, or that he was too aggressive and did not know his place, making suggestions when he had not even mastered routine work.

The next step is to analyse both points of view, to find out which one is closer to the truth. If you took the latter view, but concluded that the former was right, then it would be necessary to check and find out why you took the latter view, that is to say, why you harboured ill-feeling toward the new recruit. When you managed to trace the basic reasons for a negative way of seeing him, you might discover that the basic problem was something you never expected.

It may turn out that the basic reason for your negative view of the freshman was a reaction to criticisms you yourself received when you were new, or that it was a reflection of your antipathy for your own weakness, your inability to speak out and express your own opinions. When you have discovered the basic reasons for your own reaction, the next step is to remove this kind of negative thinking through self-reflection. Self-reflection on the path of Right View includes the whole process up to this point.

In the traditional Buddhist sense, Right View can be explained as seeing a situation according to the Four Noble Truths (The Truth of Suffering, the Truth of the Cause, the Truth of Extinction and the Truth of the Path), and as analysing things according to the law of cause and effect.

Right Thought

Second on the Noble Eightfold Path is Right Thought. Self-reflection on the path of Right Thought is analysing yourself to see if your thinking is based on Buddha's Truth. Actually, not many people are able to analyse what they think objectively, from the viewpoint of Buddha, but it could be said that if you can achieve Right Thought, 70 or even 80 per cent of the whole process of self-reflection has been completed.

Thoughts come and go in the mind all day long. It seems that all sorts of thoughts go back and forth like waves, following no particular rules or directions, but if you want to know what kind of person somebody is, it is sufficient to observe the kind of thinking that ebbs and flows in their mind.

If you want to improve yourself, the only thing you can do is to make the utmost effort to refine and purify your own thoughts. What you do is visible to others, but they cannot read your thoughts. There can be a vast gulf between the thoughts of one person and the next, and what you think and what another person thinks could be completely different. If there were a small door to your mind which could be opened with a key, so that what you were thinking was visible to others, as if on a TV screen, what kind of person you really are would be instantly revealed.

If your mind is filled with useless thoughts, just as if it were full of mental junk, it must be said that you are leading an empty life. On the other hand, if your mind is full of beautiful thoughts, it can be said that you are leading a wonderful life. In fact, improving the quality of your thoughts will ultimately lead to the purification of this world on Earth. If each person on this Earth makes an effort to refine and purify their own thoughts, it will eventually make this world a better place to live, and at the same time will contribute to eliminating hell.

The first important step you need to take is to know exactly what you are thinking, so set aside some time during the day to check what is in your own mind. If you find you have been harbouring wrong thoughts, you need to admit to this and try to correct the mistakes you have made in your thinking. Furthermore, at the end of the day, set aside some time to be quiet and reflect on the thoughts that have been in your mind. You may have restrained yourself from speaking ill of somebody. In this case, it could be said that you managed to observe the discipline of Right Speech, but if thoughts of hatred were whirling wildly inside you, this is not a desirable state, so you need to do something to correct your thoughts. If you establish a habit of regularly checking and controlling your thoughts, you will gradually be able to deepen your self-reflection.

It should be noted that in traditional Buddhism, Right Thought could be explained as having a firm resolution to continue the disciplines toward attaining enlightenment and always making correct judgements in everyday matters, on every occasion.

Right Speech

Next on the Noble Eightfold Path is Right Speech. In the section where I explained Right View, I said that having wrong views can harm our own minds. Also, we can often receive, give and spread poison through the act of speaking. In fact, the cause of a large part of human suffering is connected to words. Words spoken by others may make you suffer, while the words you speak may cause others unhappiness. Words have a lot to do with the happiness and unhappiness of human beings, and if the words that people speak are rightly 'tuned', this world on Earth will become an ideal place to live.

In the spirit world, the higher the realm a spirit belongs to, the higher the ability of the being to fine-tune their words. In the world of high spirits, it is difficult to find anyone who speaks ill of others. There may be some criticism, but when high spirits speak critically, it is principally because they want to help others, with the aim of guiding others in a better direction. In the higher spiritual realms, no one utters words of sheer hatred or resentment to another.

Words can be a very good indicator of the character of the person who utters them, so examining the kinds of words you have used during the day is a very clear and useful checkpoint for self-reflection. When you practise the discipline of Right Speech, you need to remember exactly what you said during the day. When you say something, it is usually in the presence of someone else, so remember who you came in contact with and check what you said to those you met.

If you are ill or feeling depressed, or when you are worried about something, you are more likely to utter negative words. What I mean by 'negative words' is words that will not bring others happiness, the kinds of words that hurt, that put people down, or cast a shadow over their future. Uttering negative words is tantamount to adding to the total amount of unhappiness that already exists in this world. If you are in a dark mood and feeling trapped, that is your problem alone, but once you speak out about your unhappiness, you have a negative influence on others; it is as if you are spreading the germs of unhappiness. If someone catches these negative words early on in the day, their whole day will be contaminated, and that person in turn will pass on the germs to others.

Fine-tuning the words you speak is a really important discipline. You have to speak good words, right words that are in accordance with the will of Buddha. As you continue in your discipline, fine-tuning the words that come out of your mouth, you will be led to deeper levels of self-reflection, that is to say, reflection on what you think, which is where your words originate. To explain Right Speech in a more practical manner, you need to speak truthfully, and refrain from speaking ill of others, telling lies, flattering, or saying something that plants a seed of doubt between friends.

Right Action

Traditionally, Buddhism has explained Right Action as the prohibition of criminal acts, such as killing, stealing and committing adultery, but in today's society criminal acts are controlled by a legal system. In the context of modern life I would like to interpret the concept of 'right action' as 'right work', and in this section, I would like to discuss what right work means.

In today's world, where the scale of our economic activity has grown so vast and continues to increase, it is very important to consider what the right way of working means. A crucial point to examine here is how we think about the modern value of financial profit. No economic unit can sustain its life if its income and expenditure are not in balance. This applies not only to private companies but also to public organizations, which provide administrative services based on income from taxes. The type of work characteristic of today's world is work that can be translated into profit.

In modern society, where economic values are considered

so important, what kind of life should we lead? What is a right way of working, and how should we produce new ideas? According to a traditional Buddhist way of thinking, today's business-oriented world may seem to be a place where it is quite impossible to lead a meditative life, a world in which it is difficult to practise the Noble Eightfold Path. However, it is not right to conclude hastily that we should reject this kind of world, because although such a busy world may not be conducive to a meditative life, it does contribute to the refinement and the evolution of human souls in some way or other.

If Right Action is interpreted as a right way of working, there are two very important checkpoints. The first checkpoint is to see whether the objective of your work goes against your conscience, or against your True Self. I would like you to know that before being born into this world, each and every person drew up a plan for work as an important part of their life plan. For this reason, it is important to confirm whether the occupation you are engaged in coincides with the original plan. If you discover that your job is completely out of line with your inner truth, continuing the work just to make a living will cause you a great deal of spiritual suffering. It is important to do work that is best suited to your strengths.

Much work is conducted within organizations, so assigning a role to a person who is most suited to that particular type of work within an organization is crucial. While everyone should be given equal opportunity, this does not mean that everyone should do the same job. The idea of 'putting the right man in the right place' is very useful for producing the best possible results from the whole organization, as well as from each of its members. To sum up, the first checkpoint to find out whether you are doing right work is to determine whether your work is using your aptitudes and whether or not it contradicts your own objectives in life.

The second checkpoint for work is to see whether, in doing a job, you can maintain harmonious relationships with others and whether you are adding to the happiness of others. In the world of business, of course, conflicts of interest occur between companies, but competition is justified as long as it contributes to the good of society as a whole. For example, competition between manufacturers to develop new products at lower costs will, in the long run, contribute to the development of society. If there is only one company selling a particular product that is in great demand, a monopoly can be detrimental to the public welfare, and that is why, from the perspective of Buddha's Truth, competition in a good cause is considered a good thing. A working style that causes discord in human relationships or the sort of business that is clearly harmful to the true happiness of people must be avoided. We must aim to do work that will contribute to the happiness of a greater number of people, and at the same time, when we work, we should make sure that we are in harmony with our colleagues and partners. These are the two main points we need to consider in today's society, in connection to Right Action.

7

Right Livelihood

Next, I would like to discuss self-reflection from the perspective of 'living a fulfilled life' or 'living rightly'. For each one of us, without exception, a day consists of twenty-four hours and a year of three hundred and sixty-five days. Some day, we must all leave this world on Earth; most of us will not live even to a hundred. It is more than a small portion of the day that has to be used for sleeping, for eating and for other activities necessary to fulfil the basic human requirements for sustaining life. The portion of a day that is at our disposal for work or recreation is rather limited.

It is a shocking fact that everyone in this world is given the same amount of time each day. Regardless of natural gifts and abilities, for each person a day consists of twenty-four hours, and how a person uses these hours determines the kind of life they will lead. This seems very fair for everyone. Using these twenty-four hours, some become leaders of nations, great scholars and philosophers, while others end their lives without having achieved anything positive.

Viewed from the perspective of time, this difference occurs as the result of the way people have used the time they were allotted. In this way, Right Livelihood, the fifth path of the Noble Eightfold Path, can be explained in modern terms as using each twenty-four hours, each month and each year in the right way.

I would now like to call your attention to a very important truth, that is, if we understand that time is so valuable, it is necessary to look at each day in a new light; we need to see each day as if it were our whole life, and think carefully about how we can use each twenty-four hours in the most effective way.

Most people are so optimistic they take today for granted, because they lived yesterday and they expect tomorrow will come just as today did. However, there is no guarantee that you will continue to live tomorrow. If your life were to finish today, at midnight, what would you do? How would you live? You would probably regret that you had not lived as fully as you could have.

In a nutshell, the meaning of reflection on Right Livelihood is to reflect on each day of your life, comparing it to an ideal day that you imagine you could have lived had it been the last day of your life. Through this practice, you will probably find a great deal in yourself that could be improved. The day that has just passed must have been filled with possibilities. You could have done many, many things that you were not even aware of. Imagine that you are going to die at the end of the day; then it will be easier to see if you have lived that day to the full, so you will have no regrets. In this way, reflect on what happened during the day and how you reacted to those events. Only if you continue this daily practice can you say that you are 'living rightly'.

In addition, I would like to point out that according to traditional Buddhism, making a living by criminal acts or choosing a job that is clearly against the teachings of Buddha's Truth, for example teaching materialism or preaching wrong and misleading religious beliefs, are considered violations of Right Livelihood.

8

Right Effort

Next on the Noble Eightfold Path is Right Effort, and this means making a diligent effort on the Path of Buddha's Truth. Though we tend to spend our days without thinking very carefully about the meaning of each, in actual fact each person's life has a clear destination. This is the heavenly world, where we will arrive after passing through the gateway called death. Returning to the heavenly world is a part of the scheme devised by Eternal Buddha, the Creator of the universe, to promote the evolution of human souls. To understand the true meaning of Right Effort, it is necessary to understand why this world on Earth exists. The answer is this: the three-dimensional world in which we live is a place for souls to undergo spiritual discipline to learn Truth; in other words, it is a training ground for the education of souls. Not only that, this world is also a stage on which to express the glory and prosperity of Buddha, through the expression of the great art of light. The key to understanding the meaning of Right Effort is to be found here.

There are two checkpoints that we can use to practise self-reflection on the path of Right Effort. The first is to see this world on Earth as a training ground for souls, so we need to ask ourselves whether we are making a constant effort to fulfil that objective as we live every day. In contrast to Right Livelihood, which deals with the brief span of one day, Right Effort means reflecting on yourself in the context of a longer period of time. In thinking about Right Effort, we need to see our own plan for self-development for the next year, for the next three years, five years or ten years and how we are preparing now. To summarize, the first way to practise Right Effort is to review our own lives from the standpoint of soul discipline.

The second checkpoint is to see whether we are experiencing an increase in our spirituality or an improvement of our spiritual level. The objective of the practice of Right Effort is, above all, to achieve spiritual evolution, so a way of life that does not contribute to the enhancement of our spiritual evolution should be corrected. The concept of a 'spiritual level' corresponds to the level of one's enlightenment. Then, what is meant by a higher level of enlightenment? There are three ways to assess your own level of enlightenment.

Firstly, the higher the level of enlightenment, the better you are able to see your true state. In other words, the first measurement of your own level of enlightenment is the ability to see yourself from the impartial perspective of a selfless third person, that of Buddha.

Secondly, if you have attained a higher level of enlightenment, you should be able to understand the deep connection between yourself and others, instead of seeing them as completely separate from you. In other words, you should be able to see others as friends who share the same mission to create an ideal world, or utopia on Earth.

Thirdly, at higher levels of enlightenment, you should be able to understand the meaning of human life, the reason this world exists and the reason you are allowed to live in your current environment.

When you can confirm that your understanding has improved with regard to these three aspects, it can be said that your spiritual level has become higher, and this is the very objective of the discipline of Right Effort.

Right Mindfulness

The seventh path of the Noble Eightfold Path is Right Mindfulness. If prayer is to be explained in a Buddhist way, it can be connected to Right Mindfulness and Right Concentration, which is the eighth path. In other words, prayer has attributes of both Right Mindfulness and Right Concentration. When you pray, you emit spiritual vibrations for a specific purpose, and to do that it is essential that you have attained an inner harmony and peace. So, prayer can be explained as concentrating one's will in a meditative state. It is impossible to separate prayer and self-reflection. Instead, prayer could be explained as a part of self-reflection, and if you find it difficult to understand the logic of this, it is possible to explain prayer as an applied form of self-reflection. What I would like to say is the Noble Eightfold Path does include the concept of prayer.

Now, what is the meaning of Right Mindfulness? In contrast to self-reflection on the path of Right Thought, as a way of taking control of what you think and checking every thought that has occurred in your mind, Right Mindfulness constitutes the guidelines for self-reflection on your life plan, the vision of the future that you have. The discipline of Right Mindfulness requires that you ask yourself whether the goals you hold in mind are properly set, and also what is the ideal image you have of yourself in your own mind. In a way, Right Mindfulness asks what your dreams are. If you are content to lead an ordinary life, you may just pray for the well-being of your family. On the other hand, for those who live for higher causes, life is nothing less than a series of objectives and plans so it is vitally important to set objectives and make plans carefully, to put great energy in concentrating your will on right objectives.

It could be said that the discipline of Right Mindfulness is controlling will power that is directed to a specific objective. If, for example, your will is directed to obstructing someone else's happiness or their success in a career, or causing harm to someone's business, that is obviously wrong use of will and is recorded as such in your mind. It is very important that your will be directed toward the happiness and success of as many people as possible.

The mystery of will power is that as you advance in the discipline of concentration, your will power becomes stronger, so you have to be all the more careful about controlling it. However, those who have never thought about the mystery of the power of the mind will find the discipline of Right Mindfulness to be of little significance. In this sense, it could be said that the discipline of Right Mindfulness is a highly advanced method of self-reflection.

10

Right Concentration

To conclude this chapter, I would like briefly to explain the right way to meditate. Actually, the last part of the Noble Eightfold Path, Right Concentration, is closely connected to the ultimate purpose of religion because it is the discipline of spiritual concentration, with the aim of communicating with high spirits in the other world and, further, of becoming attuned to Buddha's will and feeling it.

Without real experience of Right Concentration, you cannot claim to be spiritually awakened, or that you have perceived the true state of the world. It is not easy to know your past or future lives, but when you come into contact with high spirits through meditating rightly, and when you become aware of the great potential of your own mind, mysterious experiences await you.

The ultimate objective of Right Concentration is to acquire true wisdom and, with the power of that wisdom, to be emancipated from the fetters and chains that bind human beings to this world on Earth. Another objective of Right

Concentration is to delve deeply into your inner world. As you go deeper and deeper within, you will reach a state in which you can communicate with the guardian and guiding spirits who exist within you.

No knowledge of any kind can be truly meaningful without a spiritual backing, without the support of Buddha's Truth. No matter how well informed you may be, no matter how highly developed your intellectual abilities, without Right Concentration your personality cannot be perfected, nor will you attain great stature in a spiritual sense. As a matter of fact, many of the great figures in human history, even if they were not thought of as very religious, were in the habit of setting aside time to look deeply into the inner realms. This habit could be called a variation of the discipline of Right Concentration. These great people actually enjoyed contact with the energy that permeates the universe.

When you attain the state of Right Concentration, your potential will be maximized. The intellectual abilities of those who live on Earth are limited but all these limits are shattered when the state of Right Concentration is attained and people gain access to the great wisdom of the whole universe. With this goal in mind, I am sure you will understand that self-reflection on the path of Right Concentration means examining how completely you have recognized yourself to be a member of the universe, an integral part of the world that was created by Eternal Buddha. This state is the perfection of Right Concentration, and the perfection of your self-discipline.

When your disciplines of the Noble Eightfold Path – Right View, Right Thought, Right Speech, Right Action,

Right Livelihood, Right Effort, Right Mindfulness and Right Concentration – have been perfected, you can at least attain the state known as Arhat in the higher planes of the sixth dimension. Then a path of evolution to the beings of the seventh dimension, the Bodhisattva, will open through the further practice of putting what you have learned into action. I hope you will understand as well as being a method of self-discipline for perfecting yourself, the Noble Eightfold Path also paves the way to further development.

CHAPTER THREE

The Six Paramitas

The Innermost Wisdom

If I were to choose an idea that best characterizes Shakyamuni Buddha's teachings, it would be the idea that wisdom exists deep within the mind and wells up like a spring. In contrast to the forms of worship that emphasize prayer, Shakyamuni's original teachings were based on a belief in inner power. It should be noted, however, that in later years as Buddhism became popular and the Great Vehicle (Mahayana) movement began, followers started to worship the Buddha in heaven. This transformation from faith in the power of the self to faith in an outside power was actually supported by Shakyamuni Buddha himself in heaven.

The belief in the power of the self is based on the idea that each and every person has a source of wisdom within that is connected to the will of the universe and to the Primordial Buddha (God). The original teaching of Shakyamuni was a way for an individual to become awakened, or to evolve to a Buddha through self-discipline, so at the outset it did not include a belief in a great outside power. In other words, it could be said that early Buddhism focused on self-discipline so it did not provide a basis for the worship of an outside power. It is this aspect that distinguishes Buddhism from other religions.

Shakyamuni himself was fully aware of the existence of the Creator of the universe and he understood the power of high spirits, for he himself received various forms of guidance from them. However, in light of the way he attained enlightenment, Shakyamuni chose to teach his disciples how to go deep into the mind until they reached the wisdom within. The way of reaching deep into yourself to find the innermost wisdom and allowing it to well up is fundamental to Buddhism.

It could be said that Buddhism and Christianity were taught from two quite different perspectives. Besides the Christian idea that human beings are born sinful (although this may not have been part of the original teaching of Jesus), Buddhism seems a more advanced way of guiding people to improve themselves. In Christianity, there is no established methodology by which a human being can come closer to God. The existence of God the Father, Christ the Son, and the high spirits is clearly stated, and represented by the theology of the Holy Trinity of the Father, the Son, and the Holy Spirit. However, there is a potential risk of misleading people into believing that the masses are just like a flock of sheep, eagerly waiting to be saved. That is a sad picture of humanity.

In contrast, the human being that Buddhism describes is much stronger. Buddhism teaches that each and every person has Buddha-nature within. Shakyamuni saw the goodness and the great potential in the essential nature of human beings, independent of the physical body which is only transient. Although Buddhism includes ideas that are open to a negative interpretation, such as karma, it also has the positive concept of an infinite wisdom that exists within the human mind. This was later to develop into the teachings of the Six Paramitas.

Dana-Paramita – the perfection of offering
Sila-Paramita – the perfection of observing the precepts
Ksanti-Paramita – the perfection of perseverance
Virya-Paramita – the perfection of effort
Dhyana-Paramita – the perfection of meditation
Prajna-Paramita – the perfection of wisdom

Shakyamuni's original teachings were later compiled as the Great Vehicle philosophy which holds that, through the discipline of the Six Paramitas, a person's innermost wisdom will well up; in other words, the energy of Buddha will gush like a fountain. At this stage, human beings are described as infinitely precious because their essential nature is no different from that of Buddha.

I hope you will understand that Buddhism, from its very origin through to its development into a movement of salvation, includes the positive belief that everyone can save themselves, or, rather, is already saved.

Thoughts and Deeds

In the previous chapter, in which I described the Noble Eightfold Path, the focus was on thought, the inner activity of human beings. However, Shakyamuni did not only see human beings in connection to their inner selves, he also placed great emphasis on the relationship between thought and deed, how the one leads to the other, and whether these two are consistent.

If you really believe something, inevitably it will manifest outwardly. What is deeply inscribed in the mind will inevitably be expressed as action. In the same way, if you seek enlightenment within, what you have understood will be translated into action, and your actions in turn will speak eloquently of the kind of enlightenment you have attained. In reality, thoughts and deeds are not separate; rather, they are like two sides of a coin, so you can check whether you are living rightly in accordance with Buddha's Truth by examining both your thoughts and your actions.

How will your thoughts manifest as action? The Six

Paramitas explain how thoughts you have refined through the practice of the Noble Eightfold Path are expressed as action. The Eightfold Path and the Six Paramitas may seem to overlap, but if I were to explain the difference, I would say that the Noble Eightfold Path focuses on how to control your thoughts while the Six Paramitas demonstrate how your thoughts will be expressed in action, how an enlightened person would act.

In the end, you can only determine whether you are seeking Truth rightly through examining both the thoughts within you and your actions that are expressed in the outside world. Both in Shakyamuni's time in ancient India and today, it was and still is extremely important to know whether a particular method of self-discipline is right or wrong. You cannot determine whether a particular religious teaching is right until you have examined carefully the thoughts and actions it teaches. No matter how good the statements of a religious leader, his teachings are not worth believing if his character and behaviour are questionable, or if the core members of an order are totally corrupt. How can they set a good example to seekers of Truth? A seeker of Truth is responsible for proving his or her ability to control thoughts within through their outer expression, in other words, through actions.

Benefiting the Self
Can Benefit Others

$\mathcal{J}$n considering the teachings of Shakyamuni Buddha, the idea that 'benefiting the self can benefit others' plays a key role. Today Buddhists often say that Great Vehicle Buddhism did not start until five hundred years after Shakyamuni's death, when seekers formulated the idea of salvation and compiled the Great Vehicle sutras. One very plausible story tells how Nagarjuna went to the Real World, or the other world, in his astral travels to bring back the entire collection of scriptures and after that he started the Great Vehicle school.

Many people seem to believe that the original teachings of Shakyamuni were the Lesser Vehicle (Hinayana) doctrines that focused solely on self-improvement, while the Great Vehicle doctrines that focused on the salvation of the masses were created centuries after his death, but this is not true. Of course, many Great Vehicle sutras were compiled in later years, but most of the basic concepts of salvation had been already taught by Shakyamuni himself.

He thought, 'If refining the self means living a reclusive life, isolated from society, this sort of effort is in vain. If any self-discipline in the search for enlightenment leads only to noble isolation, what is the point of being incarnated on Earth?' When he received an offering of milk porridge from a village girl and ate it, he awakened to the fact that enlightenment was to be found in the Middle Way and that extreme asceticism did not lead to spiritual awakening. This idea integrates the concept of 'benefiting the self', which means refining oneself and enhancing a sense of happiness, and 'benefiting others', which means sharing this personal happiness with many others.

It is true that human beings are social creatures who live interacting with others. If this is the case, instead of being conceited about your own abilities, it is necessary to share what you have learned with others, with the aim of bringing them happiness. Shakyamuni had all the attributes of a good educator and his teachings quite clearly reflect this.

The main theme of this section, 'benefiting the self can benefit others', can also be explained in the following way: at the same time as you make continual efforts to develop and refine yourself, it is important to aim to make this world a better place to live, enlarging the circles of happiness, and eventually attaining great harmony between yourself and many others. Becoming exceptional must not cause discord with others; instead, your efforts to become an outstanding person must contribute to the happiness of the whole of society. In summary, the basic idea is that the sense of happiness you achieve through attaining enlightenment should be returned to society and to the people who live in it.

Both 'benefiting the self' and 'benefiting others' are important ideas, but the order of these two factors should be noted. Hidden within this sequence from self-help to helping others is a vital concept connected to the self-discipline of seekers.

While the method of self-discipline of the Noble Eightfold Path aims at attaining the state of Arhat of the sixth dimension, if you wish to go beyond this level and attain the state of Bodhisattva of the seventh dimension, it is absolutely necessary to have altruistic thoughts and put these into practice. In other words, the disciplines of self-improvement and altruism should not be separated. In the process of refining yourself, you also have to sow seeds that will grow to benefit others. That is a very important requirement for becoming a Bodhisattva. It explains the reason why those who pursued a Zen training in an isolated world of self-satisfaction could not reach a state beyond that of the sixth dimension.

The teaching of the Six Paramitas is a bridge between the state of Bodhisattva and that of Tathagata. It is also a method in which the Noble Eightfold Path is further developed into guidelines for conduct for those who aim to reach the state of Bodhisattva and beyond. In the following sections, I would like to explain each of the Six Paramitas in detail.

Dana-Paramita (the Perfection of Offering)

The first discipline of the Six Paramitas is 'Dana-Paramita', which is also called 'the perfection of offering'. The teachings on offering are a very important part of Shakyamuni's teachings. Offering is a Buddhist way of expressing love, and it is similar to the Christian idea of charity. The fact that the perfection of offering is the first discipline of the Six Paramitas proves how much importance Shakyamuni placed on the idea of love, or, more specifically, compassion for others.

Now, let me briefly explain the term 'Paramita'. This Sanskrit word originally meant reaching the other shore, or attaining the state of emancipation. It can also mean 'when you go deeply into the well within, an abundant wisdom will flow out.' Accordingly, 'Dana-Paramita' can be explained as the discipline of offering, through which you can fully appreciate and assimilate the wisdom that wells up from within.

There are many different types of offerings. Most common is the offering of material wealth – for instance clothes, property or precious objects – to mendicant seekers, to religious orders or to the poor. Offering something to another is certainly an act of love, and even if you cannot give material things, you can still give a smile. A smile on your face can help make this world a better place to live.

Offering the Law is a more advanced, spiritual level of offering. The act of offering the Law, in other words, teaching the Truth, is the best offering for those who are spiritually needy; like parched and sandy ground they crave the Truth to quench their thirst. In the time of Shakyamuni, lay people would make a habit of offering things to monks and nuns, but they in turn would receive much more than they had given. The mendicants expressed their gratitude to lay people through their loving act of offering the Law. When lay followers explained Buddha's Truth to others who were not yet awakened to faith, this act was also considered an offering of the Law.

Another type of offering is to offer peace of mind to those who are frightened, suffering or in pain by helping them solve their troubles. Offering material wealth, offering the Law and offering peace of mind are called the Three Offerings.

Sila-Paramita (the Perfection of Observing the Precepts)

Next of the Six Paramitas is 'Sila-Paramita', which is also called 'the perfection of observing the precepts'. Many people probably associate self-discipline with some sort of precepts or with a stoical lifestyle; this applies not only to Buddhism but also to other religions. Islam, for example, has extremely strict precepts, and Christianity has a set of rules for the conduct of monks and nuns. The purpose of religious precepts is to protect seekers of the Truth from various worldly temptations.

It is not easy for ordinary people to understand what right thought or right action is, so certain guidelines were established to prevent them from committing sins, so that they could at least satisfy the minimum requirements. Shakyamuni regarded the precepts as a very important means of educating people, because, unless they were given certain rules of conduct, seekers had difficulty controlling their behaviour.

The main requirement of the discipline of Sila-Paramita is that the following five precepts are observed: do not kill, do not steal, do not commit adultery, do not speak falsely and do not drink.

The precept 'do not kill', teaching people that killing is a sin, comes first because in Shakyamuni's time, murder was quite common.

Next is 'do not steal'. Stealing means not only taking the possessions of another by force but also taking things that you are not allowed to possess. An act of stealing may benefit the one who steals but it causes others harm, disturbing their peace of mind and creating social disorder. This precept was formulated to avoid this.

The next precept is 'do not commit adultery', do not have affairs outside a celebrated marriage. There are two reasons that extramarital affairs are wrong. Firstly, they destroy the family, which is the basic building block of society. Secondly, they intensify sensuous desire and prevent the seeker from concentrating on the path to enlightenment. For these reasons, this precept was put in place.

In the case of kings and maharajahs, however, having more than one wife was socially acceptable; it was not considered a violation of the precept 'do not commit adultery'. Unlike Christianity, Buddhism did not traditionally stipulate monogamy, and if a relationship was based on love and if sufficient financial support was provided, it was acceptable to have more than one wife to satisfy the need to uphold social status. This was actually connected to the fact that Shakyamuni Buddha accepted as his followers many members of royal families.

Next is the precept 'do not speak falsely'. This includes telling lies, speaking ill of others and slander. To say something with the express intention of catching someone out was prohibited. Even among the members of Shakyamuni's order, there was no end of people who spoke ill of others or envied fellow seekers whose level of enlightenment was more advanced. These unfortunate circumstances were the grounds for the prohibition of speaking falsely.

The last of the five main Buddhist precepts is 'do not drink'. People might argue about whether drinking alcoholic beverages is good or bad, and in fact, at times some high spirits in heaven do enjoy the sensation of drinking, so the habit of drinking cannot be flatly condemned. However, it should be noted that in Shakyamuni's time alcohol in India was of very bad quality and caused terrible intoxication, and drinkers were usually thought of as lazy.

In any case, it is true to say that drinking definitely interferes with concentration and tends to undermine people's desire for self-improvement. Because of this, the precept against drinking was established to maintain social order. This precept also involved the element of encouragement for seekers to continue on the path of self-discipline and fight worldly temptations and desires.

These were the precepts that were commonly observed at the time of Shakyamuni, but in today's world, many of these actions are restricted by law, so now it may be necessary to create other precepts for seekers of Truth.

Ksanti-Paramita (the Perfection of Perseverance)

Next comes 'Ksanti-Paramita', which is also called 'the perfection of perseverance'. Following the virtue of offering and the virtue of observing the precepts was the virtue of perseverance.

When I look at the life of Shakyamuni, it seems to me that perseverance played an important role. In order to develop ourselves, to achieve spiritual improvement over a long period of time, perseverance is absolutely essential, and this is the very reason that seekers of Truth were taught the discipline of Ksanti-Paramita.

A lack of patience often gives rise to frustration that disturbs a person's peace of mind, and this then gives rise to discord in human relations. When you become fully aware that the key to victory in life is 'perseverance', you will find you have reached an advanced spiritual level.

The meaning of the discipline of Ksanti-Paramita can be summarized in the following four points.

The first is a warning against impatience. Seekers of Truth tend to become impatient with their progress, comparing themselves with others, because of a desire to become enlightened before them. However, it takes an extremely long time to attain enlightenment. Because of the very fact that they are seekers, they must endure the pain of not being able to attain enlightenment for a long time. The moment they lose patience, they will begin to stray from the right path.

The second point is tolerance, not only putting up with situations that seem to be against you, but also letting go of feelings of resentment. When we attempt to study Truth and convey it to others, we often become a subject of criticism and accusations. In fact, the more authentic the teaching, the more intense the enemy attack will tend to be, because the world is full of wrong thoughts and evil actions, and the spread of authentic teachings will obstruct the force of evil. When this occurs, a seeker of Truth must not take in the poison of the attack, but instead overcome the difficulties quietly, continuing to walk steadily on the right path. It is important for a seeker to hold to this attitude.

The third point is endurance in the face of objections from family or relatives. When people decide to walk the path of Truth while living in this world on Earth, it is as if they sever their connection with the past, once and for all. After this major turning point, their life will completely change, and those who are close to them may start complaining, or try to persuade them to go back on their decision. Although they do this out of love, it is a worldly love stemming from a lack of more exalted spiritual knowledge. What they think of as 'common sense' will inevitably stand in the way of the seeker, and it becomes even more important to endure and maintain peace of mind.

The fourth point is endurance against evil. In the process of striving for enlightenment, a seeker will have to confront trial by various evil spirits and devils. Shakyamuni himself was tested by the devil Mara Papiyas, and Jesus was tempted by Beelzebub. In the same way, the interference of the force of evil is inevitable for a seeker of Truth, because the greater the number of people that become enlightened, the larger the territory that will be taken from evil spirits. To prevent this, they will, out of an instinct to defend, try to obstruct the Light.

In such circumstances, it becomes vital to endure the attack of the enemy and overcome the difficulties. The discipline of developing oneself and increasing one's inner light may seem a passive approach, and you may be tempted to cut the devils out with the swing of sword, but you should make an effort to continue to endure tirelessly, to make it through and come out the other side. When a seeker walks on the path toward the Light, before becoming truly enlightened, trial by evil is inevitable, and this is the reason that endurance is absolutely essential for the seeker.

7

Virya-Paramita (the Perfection of Effort)

The 'Virya-Paramita' is also called 'the perfection of effort', and it is the discipline of making an effort. In the Noble Eightfold Path there is also the path of Right Effort and in the end the meaning of the two is the same but Virya-Paramita places more importance on the actual practice of working toward an objective that has been clearly set. This discipline requires the setting of clear goals and continuing in an actual practice to reach those goals. It is the accumulation of daily effort to fulfil clear objectives, for example, making offerings, doing meditation, or explaining the Law, in such a way that others can confirm your achievements. In terms of the study of the Law, it is also important to assess how much progress you have made every day. In this way, in the discipline of Virya-Paramita, precise goals have to be set, and in fact many of Shakyamuni's disciples continued the discipline of attaining these goals.

One of the outstanding characteristics of Shakyamuni's order was that its members studied very diligently, and this distinguished them from the followers of other religions. In those days, the worship of supernatural powers was very strong and many people had a strong desire to get into the limelight by demonstrating their extraordinary powers. In contrast, although Shakyamuni respected communication with the spiritual realms, at the same time he expected his followers to be respected in all walks of society, to possess common sense and the ability to make sound judgements. For this reason, members of the order were strongly motivated and enthusiastic in their study of Buddha's Law. This strong enthusiasm for study helped Shakyamuni's disciples to build a balanced foundation of knowledge based on Truth and also assisted character development.

It is often said that those who continue to study will eventually acquire great stature. In fact, the aim of studying is not only to acquire knowledge; the very process of making a diligent effort to achieve a clear objective in any field of study also contributes to the development of character. For this reason, it is not surprising that those who diligently study Buddha's Truth, the most important of all studies, will refine themselves and become outstanding people.

The virtue of effort was an important part of Shakyamuni's teachings, and any teaching that neglects effort – for example, one that says 'anyone can become enlightened quite naturally, without making any effort' or 'if you simply pray, you will be blessed by divine grace' – was rejected. It should be remembered that the fact that Shakyamuni put great emphasis on making a constant effort contributed to raising the level of his disciples' study of the Law.

8

Dhyana–Paramita (the Perfection of Meditation)

The discipline of 'Dhyana-Paramita' is also called 'the perfection of meditation'. It overlaps Right Concentration of the Noble Eightfold Path, but the difference between these two types of discipline can be found in their focus. While Right Concentration focuses on examining one's state of mind when meditating, checking that it is right, Dhyana-Paramita focuses on continuing the daily practice of meditation.

When you have spare time, for instance at the weekend, it is probably not so difficult to reflect on yourself, to go deep within and examine your past thoughts and actions. On the other hand, it is not easy to do this in the same way when you are constantly on the move; then, it takes a great effort. So, it could be said that anyone who has continued to set aside time for introspection every day has already succeeded in achieving something extraordinary.

I would like you to think about your own situation. It may not be so difficult to remember what has happened in your life from the time you were born. But do you realize how difficult it is to continue discovering, investigating and getting to know your inner self on a daily basis? It actually takes extraordinary effort.

The ultimate goal of Dhyana-Paramita is to be in a constant state of meditation, not only when you are following a formal method of meditation practice, but also when you are working or doing other things in daily life. In other words, the perfection of 'Dhyana-Paramita' means attaining a meditative state no matter what you are doing, whether you are walking, speaking or working. At this perfected level, every minute of your twenty-four hours is spent in a state of meditation; your thoughts are constantly directed to the heavenly world and you can communicate with high spirits at any time. This is the highest state of mind that seekers of Truth should aim to achieve through discipline.

Today followers of Zen Buddhism practise meditation sitting cross-legged in temples in the remotest places. When we are detached from our daily lives it is not so difficult to penetrate our inner world deeply, but in everyday working life it is extremely hard to maintain a meditative state.

When this highest state of meditation is achieved, the mind is perfectly calm. Even if someone attacks you, using abusive language, it does not disturb the serenity within, and it is as if there is an inner lake with a still surface, like a mirror. Living in such a perfected state is exactly the same as being in the heavenly world while still on Earth. In other words, this is the perfection of Dhyana-Paramita that seekers work hard to attain. It is like living in the higher planes of the Real World, such as the Bodhisattva Realm (the seventh dimension) or the Tathagata Realm (the eighth dimension), while still in this world. This state was one of the objectives most desired by the members of Shakyamuni's order.

Prajna-Paramita (the Perfection of Wisdom)

The last of the Six Paramitas is 'Prajna-Paramita'. The word 'Prajna' means deep wisdom, not just superficial knowledge. It can also be translated as transcendental wisdom, which wells up from deep within like an inexhaustible spring. When you attain transcendental wisdom, true knowledge is sieved from all the knowledge you have acquired and the experiences you have been through in this earthly world; it is as if gold dust is sieved out.

To become someone of great stature, much reading and experience in the world is required. As you continue in your efforts, the knowledge and experience you have gained will start to shine like precious gems. However, when transcendental wisdom has been attained, it gives out such a brilliant light that these gems of worldly knowledge and experience appear duller than before. Transcendental wisdom is so precious for it only wells up when a window of the mind has been opened.

As you continue to make an effort to attain a right state of mind through the practice of the Noble Eightfold Path, at some point your mind will become spiritually open and you will start to communicate with your own guardian and guiding spirits. The wisdom of guardian and guiding spirits in the Real World is far greater than the wisdom of people on Earth, because spirits in the Real World have access to all the knowledge that they gained and all the experiences they had in past incarnations.

While we live in this world on Earth, we are only able to use about 10 per cent of the resources from our past lives, and the rest remains latent. However, when we return to the Real World, the latent 90 per cent comes to the fore as our surface consciousness, while the consciousness from the most immediate past life becomes subconscious. So according to a simple calculation, if the spiritual level of a spirit in heaven and a person on Earth is the same, essentially the spirit in heaven has nine times as much wisdom as the counterpart on Earth.

Needless to say, in the Real World there are many spiritual beings who are probably far more advanced than you. There is a constellation of all the wisest sages who we cannot see on Earth in this era. A doctor or a professor who is supposedly at the highest level of intelligence in today's world would probably not be superior to Socrates, and none of today's philosophers could possibly be of a higher calibre than Confucius.

The Real World is filled not only with great figures from history, but also with high spirits who played important roles in civilizations that existed beyond human recall. When innumerable spiritual beings join forces to guide those who live on Earth, how much power could worldly knowledge and endeavour possibly have in comparison?

High spirits in heaven are sending me inspiration, and the wisdom exhibited in their guidance far exceeds the knowledge that can be acquired in this world on Earth. It could be said that receiving inspiration from the high spirits is another way in which Prajna-Paramita is practised.

It is important to know that the ultimate objective of making an effort in this life is to attain the highest level of wisdom that one can. If you truly understand Buddha's Truth, the wisdom you attain will bring you emancipation and transform you into a person of immense power.

10

A Modern Interpretation of the Six Paramitas

Following the explanation of the idea of the Six Paramitas, in this last section I would like to explore how we can practise the Six Paramitas in our daily lives. The Six Paramitas have a lot in common with the Noble Eightfold Path, and I would like to cast some light on these six disciplines from a new angle.

First, I would like to describe 'Dana-Paramita' as loving acts. In other words, this is the practice of 'love that gives'.

In an attempt to apply the spirit of 'Sila-Paramita' to modern life, I would like to express it as a revival of stoicism in its original Greek sense. When you simplify your life and seek intellectual and spiritual values in the plain lifestyle of a stoic, you are observing Sila-Paramita. Those who have exalted goals and make a constant effort on the path to their objective find no need to be pretentious. They live a stoical lifestyle in today's society, concentrating their energy on the pursuit that is most important to them while remaining unconcerned with minor, worldly matters. This is what I mean by a stoicism that can be practised in today's society.

The practice of 'Ksanti-Paramita' could be described as an attitude of waiting patiently until the time is ripe, while building your strength. When you are experiencing difficult times, it is important to wait for the right time, while continuing to develop your abilities, just as if you are waiting patiently for a jar to fill up with drips of water, instead of trying to do something ill-thought-out. This is the way to observe the spirit of Ksanti-Paramita.

'Virya-Paramita' means making a diligent effort, and I would like modern-day seekers to focus on making an effort to explore and study Buddha's Truth.

'Dhyana-Paramita' can be connected to the practice of the Noble Eightfold Path as a part of daily life. I intend to continue giving you simple explanations of the Noble Eightfold Path in many different ways, because the setting aside of time to be silent and to practice self-reflection is important. This practice will be accomplished as the path of reflection, part of the Fourfold Path (of love, knowledge, reflection and development) which is the main pillar of my teaching today at the Institute for Research in Human Happiness (IRH).

Lastly, 'Prajna-Paramita' corresponds to the second path of the Fourfold Path, the path of knowledge. It is my intention to compile a system of spiritual wisdom that exists in the Real World, or the other world, and to this end, I will continue to publish books of Buddha's Truth.

On a personal level, some of you may experience spiritual communication with your guardian spirit once you have unlocked the door to the spirit world. As you continue your discipline to rid your mind of dark clouds, you may at a certain point receive inspiration from your guardian spirit, and this is proof that you have been successful.

It could be said that the other five disciplines – the practice of love that gives, leading the lifestyle of a stoic, perseverance, diligent effort in study and setting aside time for self-reflection – play the important role of protecting those who have opened a spiritual window from going astray. I will conclude my explanation of the Six Paramitas in the context of modern life here.

CHAPTER FOUR

The Idea of
the Void

What Does it Mean to be Human?

In this chapter, I would like to explore the Buddhist concept of the void. To understand this, it is essential to understand the Buddhist view of human beings, of life and death and of the world. Without clarifying these points, it is difficult to discuss the idea of the void.

The first question is 'What does it mean to be human?' In answer to this question, Shakyamuni defined the human being in a revolutionary way. At that time in India, the prevailing belief was that a human being was born with a burden of karma, that a person's social status was predestined and their fate already determined at the time of birth. In contrast to this, Shakyamuni argued that 'there is a flow of destiny determined by the law of karma and other factors that you cannot control, but there is also a way of overcoming destiny, and that is through the spiritual disciplines for attaining enlightenment.'

This new idea that Shakyamuni introduced was very good news for the masses of those times. In today's world, people perhaps tend to think that Buddhism is an austere teaching that views the world in a pessimistic way, but for people of those times, Shakyamuni's teachings were encouraging and quite revolutionary.

Under its rigid caste system, Indian society in Shakyamuni's time was divided into four classes. There was the Brahman, the priest caste; Kshatriya, the warrior caste; Vaisya, the merchant caste: and Sudra, the slave caste. Further, there were people regarded as lower than Sudra; they belonged to the Chandala, a caste who were not even considered human and were treated like cattle or rather worse because they were regarded as unclean. Those who were born into such a low class remained powerless, without any possibility of improving their lot through their own efforts. Birth into a Chandala caste determined their fate and there was nothing they could do about it. On the other hand, those born into the Brahman caste were automatically recognized as members of the officiating priest caste, no matter what kind of people they were. Shakyamuni sharply questioned this reality.

Shakyamuni thought that Eternal Buddha, the great wisdom that governs the entire universe, would not tolerate a situation like this, and that something must be done to overcome the class system. To this end, he set out to create a new values system within his order where, regardless of their class determined at birth, seekers were given an equal opportunity to practise self-discipline and attain enlightenment. Regardless of birth, the members of Shakyamuni's order were all seekers, and they were given a new status, a new goal and a new reason to live; this was the ideal state that Shakyamuni envisioned.

This is similar to what we are now attempting to do at the Institute for Research in Human Happiness that I head, aiming to create a new values system based on Buddha's Truth. The activities of the Institute are directed toward creating a system in which studying Buddha's Truth and becoming spiritually awakened is held in the highest regard.

In the same way, Shakyamuni saw great significance in emancipating those who believed that happiness was out of their reach. This ideal was realized through the creation of a new values system, a complete change in values within a rigid, caste-based society. Shakyamuni brought people the wonderful news that they could open up a path to true happiness through the practice of self-discipline. The condition for making this ideal a reality was, first of all, to aspire to become enlightened, then the actual practice of the disciplines was required.

The Meaning of
Life and Death

Next, I would like to look at the Buddhist views of life and death. When Shakyamuni was living, India was ravaged by continual wars and attacks by neighbouring countries were a constant menace, so people could not take it for granted that they would live to see the next day. The Kapilavastu palace where Shakyamuni was brought up eventually went to rack and ruin. Even Shakyamuni, the Great Spirit from the ninth dimension, was not capable of protecting his own country and people. Everything was transient.

In those days, 'living' had the negative connotation of winning battles. In order to sustain their own lives, people had to kill enemies, and only those who were prepared to live even at the cost of the others' lives could survive, and the rest had no choice but to perish. Being a pacifist or being without power meant certain death. Against this backdrop, it is hardly surprising that people generally felt that life was futile, and yearned strongly for a world after death. They even despised the negative idea of 'living'.

It is true that even among those who aspired to enlightenment, there were many who longed for happiness in the next life rather than the attainment of Buddhahood on Earth. They wished to return to a world of happiness after leaving this life, which for them was nothing but suffering.

For that reason, Shakyamuni incorporated a belief in the next life in his teachings. At a time when life was so full of ugliness, of suffering and sadness because of the circumstances, there was a need to preach faith in the next life. Preaching to people of a yearning for the next life may have been like anaesthetic for them, but it worked well, freeing them for even a brief spell from the anguish and suffering they could never escape.

Reincarnation

In connection with any discussion of the meaning of life and death, the idea of reincarnation is very important. Other major religions, namely Christianity, Islam, Judaism, Confucianism and Taoism, do not describe the concept of reincarnation as clearly as Buddhism does, so it is one of the major features of Buddhism.[1] Indeed, the fact that Shakyamuni taught this concept explicitly contributed to the spread of his teachings, and why they have such vast influence in today's world. This is proof that Buddhism is indeed a teaching of Truth.

Can you imagine how much courage it took Shakyamuni to declare publicly such an extraordinary idea as reincarnation? In today's world, the idea is known as a part of Buddhism so people probably do not find it far-fetched, but can you imagine the difficulty of telling people they had lived before and would reincarnate again in future, when they had absolutely no idea about this? Because the idea of reincarnation is connected to the mechanism of a world nobody can see, hear or validate, many people found it hard to accept.

In India in Shakyamuni's time, belief in reincarnation was a form of religious faith. The general feeling of people was 'Because Shakyamuni said so, I will try to believe it.' Not many people were totally convinced by the concept of reincarnation, but generally they accepted the idea because they respected and trusted Shakyamuni.

The idea of reincarnation itself was not unique to Buddhism. Even the folk religions of India in those days spoke of the transmigration of soul, but in many cases it was about transformations from human to animal form, to even lizards and pigeons. The concept that a human soul could transmigrate into all sorts of animals contributed to promoting an awareness of animal protection and enhancing compassion for life, but it was not a law that could be universally applied. Yet Shakyamuni, who was a very good teacher and storyteller, used the deer, the pigeon and other life forms, as an expedient way to help people understand the concept of human reincarnation.

In reality, however, human souls have been distinctively human for hundreds of millions of years. There is very little possibility of human souls being born in the bodies of animals. Humans always reincarnate as humans, except in very rare cases where a human soul experiences a life as an animal for a brief period for the purpose of special training. This occurs only in the bodies of highly evolved animals, and only for the duration of a year or two. This kind of special training is arranged to teach people what a precious opportunity it is to be born human. It means that some domestic animals like dogs and cats may have been human in the past, and because they still possess human senses, living in an animal body is an excruciating experience. When a difficult life of this kind is over, these souls will have realized how wonderful it is to be human, but, as I said earlier, this only occurs rarely and as an exception.

An understanding of reincarnation brings about a revolutionary change in our perspective of life. A large proportion of human suffering occurs because people think they only live once. When they become fully aware that this present life is only one point in the eternal flow of time, and that they have lived in the past and will live again in the future, they will understand that their future lives will depend on their present life and also that they can choose what kind of life they will live in the future.

Consequently, if you wish to live happily in the world after death, or in your next incarnation, you need to sow the seeds of happiness now. This means that you can make preparations for a fulfilling life in the future through your own efforts. In fact, the idea of reincarnation guarantees you a reward for the efforts you make now. It is just like savings which promise a large return in years to come. In this way, the idea of reincarnation helps guide people in a positive direction because it encourages them to make an effort now. This effort is never wasted, but guarantees them a return in the future.

The Discovery of the Real World

I have discussed the Buddhist views of human existence, of life and death, and reincarnation, and now I would like to talk on the subject of how Shakyamuni recognized the other world, or the Real World.

After Shakyamuni's order grew to be an organization of several thousand followers, Shakyamuni would give sermons once a week to a congregation; the rest of the week he limited his activities to a few meetings with leading disciples. In this way, he was able to secure ample time for meditation. While meditating outdoors, his mind would often leave his body and he would travel to the Real World.

Shakyamuni's understanding of the Real World was quite advanced at that time. Already he could comprehend the nature of the ninth-dimensional Cosmic Realm, that it is limited not only to the sphere surrounding planet Earth but is also connected to the realms surrounding other planets. He was aware that there are highly advanced spirits on other planets, and that they too are undergoing spiritual discipline to improve themselves.

When he experienced the infinite expansion of his spiritual self to the extent that he identified himself with the entire universe, he felt this planet Earth shrink to a tiny dot, as small as one of the cells in an internal organ. Through this experience, he could understand how it felt to be the universe itself, but it was extremely difficult to explain such things to his disciples. At that time in India, people were not prepared to learn about the structure of the universe, so he just spoke of it metaphorically.

In my book *The Laws of Eternity*, I have clarified the structure of the Real World, but some two thousand five hundred years ago Shakyamuni had the same knowledge, although his understanding was limited to the framework of the prevailing thoughts in ancient India. If I were to point to any lack in his perception, it would be that in astral travel to the Real World, he could only contact those who belonged to Indian territory because his view of the world did not extend beyond India. It was very difficult for him to contact those inhabiting other areas of the spirit world. He also observed many spirits with various lifestyles he thought peculiar, but he did not go as far as exploring where they belonged, or what kind of lives they led. However, it was true that his actual experiences of the Real World through astral travel helped him a great deal when he taught on the meaning of life and death, the purpose of human life, and reincarnation. His discovery of the Real

World contributed an additional height, depth and authenticity to his thoughts.

Shakyamuni's experience of the Real World was similar to my own, in that I contacted a variety of spirits and then published their messages. I believe that the publication of my books of spiritual messages has helped people to accept the existence of the Real World that many high spirits inhabit, and has laid the foundations for the publication of my books on the Laws of Buddha's Truth.

Religion after all is nothing other than the science of the Real World. Any spiritual teaching that does not have the backing of a knowledge of the Real World should be called a philosophy. It would not be an exaggeration to say that the difference between philosophy and religion is the commitment on the part of religion to explore the Real World in a scientific manner.

Looking Anew at the Physical World

When you become aware of the existence of the Real World, how does this three-dimensional physical world look? To answer this, it may help to think of overseas travel. When you go to a foreign country for the first time in your life, you experience a life and culture that are different from what you have been used to. If you have had a one-year stay in a place that is blessed with an abundant natural environment, on returning home to a big city you may experience the once familiar density of population or the narrow streets congested with traffic as somewhat strange.

Similarly, once you have known what the Real World is like, the way people live in this world on Earth may seem odd. This feeling of strangeness stems partly from the difference in values. From the perspective of heaven, the way people live on Earth, working away busily day after day, makes them look like ants carrying granules of sugar. These ants are toiling at the task of collecting food which they probably believe is the supreme objective of their lives, but looked at from above, their efforts may seem quite futile. Similarly, when you awaken to the values of the Real World, this material world may appear empty and transient.

However, this is only at the first stage in looking at this world in a spiritual way. Next, it is necessary to ask why such a transient and futile world should exist. As you contemplate this question deeply and try to understand the true meaning of this world, you will realize that behind its transient appearances, the circumstances of this world have been provided for us as important materials for learning, to help our spiritual discipline. Furthermore, you will become aware that the physical body and the things of this world are not in conflict with spiritual values. Both spirit and matter are composed of the same elements; it is simply that they manifest differently.

The spirit is composed of Buddha's Light, and the material things of this world are also the manifestations of His energy. It is just like the different forms that water takes; when water vapour is cooled it turns into a liquid form which, when frozen, then turns into a solid form, ice. Water and ice look different, but they are simply different manifestations of the same substance.

When your perception of the world deepens and you go beyond the stage where you feel the contrast of the material world with the spiritual world, you will understand that both this world and the other are essentially the same, but that they manifest differently. When you reach this level of understanding, you will experience a complete turnaround in your perceptions of this world on Earth, from negative to positive. You will be able to read the grand plan designed by Eternal Buddha in the things of this world.

The Buddhist Idea of the Void

The theme of the last section, 'looking anew at the physical world', is actually connected to the Buddhist idea of 'the void'. You have probably heard the phrase 'matter is void, void is matter' from the Heart Sutra. This is considered one of the most important sayings in Buddhism, and in turn, knowing this phrase can make people feel they have understood Buddhism.

There are two levels to an understanding of the idea of the void. The first level of understanding is to distinguish this world from the other world. In the phrase 'matter is void', 'matter' implies this world on Earth, so the phrase means this world is transient and has come into being only temporarily; only the other world is real. Everything in this world perishes. Each and every person, whether of humble or noble birth, will eventually die. Their bodies will perish and only the soul will return to the Real

World. 'Matter' which is visible to our eyes exists only temporarily. It will change and eventually disappear into the Real World, and because the Real World is invisible, it is described by the expression 'the void'.

On the other hand, 'void is matter' implies that spirits in the Real World incarnate into this world for the purpose of spiritual discipline. They go through the cycle of reincarnation over and over again, to experience life in a physical body. Because the meaning of incarnation is the transition from an invisible to a visible state, it is described in the phrase 'void is matter'.

In this way, at the first level of understanding, the idea of the void describes the difference between this world and the other, and the cycle of reincarnation between this world and the other. But there is a higher level of understanding, and it is connected to the question, 'What is the essential nature of the most basic element that constitutes both the things of this world and of the other?'

To answer this question, I would like to introduce a philosophy that says everything is composed of Buddha's Light. I teach that the world has a multi-layered structure, ranging from the third to the ninth dimension, but ultimately only Light exists. Only the Light is real. Buddha's Light transforms itself to create the various states of the world, both material and spiritual. In the spirit world, the spiritual body and the light body that is enveloped within it are made of Light. When Buddha's Light manifests itself in this three-dimensional world, first the most basic particles are created, then these 'spiritons' collect to form the elementary particles that physics talks of, which in turn form materials of all sorts.

This way of looking at the world is in accordance with the leading edge of modern physics, which has discovered that elementary particles have the attributes of both particles and waves. This seemingly contradictory characteristic becomes natural when we consider the truth that everything in this world, both material and spiritual, is a manifestation of Buddha's Light.

In this way, the spiritual energy of Buddha's Light creates matter in this world, and when something material breaks up, it dissolves again into spiritual energy. This concept of the circulation of energy and matter is the explanation of the idea of the void in the phrase 'matter is void; void is matter'. Advances in modern science have made it possible to explain the void in the context of physics.

Why is the Idea of the Void Important?

My previous discussion of the concept of the void now leads to the following questions: 'Why is the idea of the void so important?' 'Why has Buddhism raised the question of the void?' 'Why does it talk about a world nobody can see?' 'Why does the invisible turn into the visible, and the visible into the invisible?' In this section, I would like to attempt to answer these questions.

These kinds of questions are in fact connected to the origin of the Zen sect of Buddhism. There is a practice called the 'Zen dialogue', a dialogue that is based on an unconventional question; its aim is to awaken the seeker who is attempting to answer the question to his or her Buddha-nature, and to the truth that the Real World exists. The idea behind this practice is that through the contemplation of a theme totally unconnected to your present situation, you will be awakened to your true being and to your attitudes, as if you are looking into a mirror. So it could be said that this rather strange theme, the void, gave rise to the emergence of the Zen schools in later years, although Zen thought as it exists now is the result of a deviation from the original teachings of Shakyamuni.

When you think about the reason that people become attached to the things of this world, you will understand it is because they can see this world and they think it is real. They become attached to the physical body because they can see it. Seeing members of the opposite sex may lead to attachments, and the same can be said about food. However, when people are attached to things, there can be no peace of mind. Only when they are rid of their attachments can they enjoy serenity within, which gives rise to a sense of true happiness. Shakyamuni was fully aware of this truth, so he taught the idea 'matter is void'.

He said, 'Listen, all monks and nuns. You may think that the things of this world that are visible to your eyes – your body, matter and all living things in nature – are real and substantial, but they exist only temporarily. Their real state is only void'. Can you imagine the magnitude of the shock these monks and nuns experienced?

However, anyone who has looked at a substance through an electron microscope will understand the truth 'matter is void.' What seems to our eyes to be solid when magnified reveals itself to be an aggregate of particles which have a lot of space between them. The things of this world, which to our eyes appear real, turn out to be mere illusion.

The reason that Shakyamuni taught the idea of the void

117

was that he intended to free people's minds, minds that tended to be attached to the things of this Earth, and to awaken them to the world of true values. This first stage of negation has something in common with the ideas that are fundamental to Zen. However, to teach 'matter is void' only would be rather one-sided, the other side of the truth, 'void is matter' also needs to be taught.

To explain the idea 'void is matter', Shakyamuni stated, 'All things on this Earth are created by the Will of Eternal Buddha. Although you can neither see nor touch this, when it manifested as the word, the word took on concrete form and came into being in this world. This planet called Earth, and all the animals and plants on it, came into being through the Will of Eternal Buddha. This world was created by His Will, and by the work of a multitude of high spirits who devoted themselves to conveying His Will to people.' Shakyamuni taught that matter is void and also that void is matter. This kind of well-balanced perspective is an important characteristic of Shakyamuni's thought.

To summarize, the idea of the void was taught firstly as a method of spiritual practice, to rid people of attachments to this world, but also as a way of instructing them about the origin of this world and human life, to reveal the secrets of Creation. Because of those two aims, the teaching of the void has been considered very important.

8

All Things are Transient

In relation to this idea of the void, there is the well-known ancient idea that 'all things are transient'. In classical Japanese literature, this expression appears at the beginning of 'The Tale of Heike', the famous war chronicle of the Heike clan, written in the thirteenth century. There is a certain strain of sadness in this expression, and one cannot help but feel the pathos of the vanquished and the dying. The author seems to be saying that he sees transience in the rise and fall of powerful clans.

When we consider the idea that 'all things are transient' in the context of Shakyamuni's thought in India over two thousand years ago, we see the steadfast perspective of a person who was fully aware of the existence of the Real World. 'All things are transient' does not only imply the ever-changing nature of existence in this world from the perspective of someone living on Earth. It also implies the observation of the ever-changing vicissitudes of human affairs on Earth from the viewpoint of the Real World.

Only those who have fully grasped the unchanging within this ever-changing world can ever understand the true meaning of this world. All human deeds will be washed away in the merciless passage of time, only to disappear. History is like the flow of a river that carries away all human endeavour, and only those who are awakened to the immutable in the midst of change will be able to understand the futility of the passing of this world in the truest sense.

The idea of the transience of all things was never intended to be a pessimistic way of looking at life. It is a description of the state of this world from the viewpoint of the Real World, and it is still true. When you truly awaken to the world of Buddha's Truth, you may feel that the world of business is meaningless. No matter how many volumes of literature you read, you may feel that there is nothing more than a barren desert. In the face of the vast ocean of Buddha's Truth, all the things of this world are like bubbles in the sea that are bound to disappear. So unless you continue to learn what is of true spiritual value, and absorb what is nourishing to your soul, you will never understand the true meaning of living on this Earth.

In summarizing this discussion of the phrase 'all things are transient', I would like to say that this idea should not be understood simply as a pessimistic way of seeing life. It means that those who are able to look at this world from the perspective of the Real World may experience moments when things they used to find attractive and of great value lose their magic. When you are awakened to the values of the Real World, days spent in competition for promotion or in pursuit of love affairs will seem worthless. However, you must remember that this realization is only the first step toward enlightenment.

9

The Void and Nothingness

There is another concept very similar to the idea of the void, that is the idea of nothingness. This is a vast subject in itself and it would perhaps require a book to discuss it in detail, so in this section I would like to give just a brief explanation of this idea.

The void and nothingness seem similar, but do they mean the same thing? As I have explained, the void does not mean that nothing exists; rather, it implies an ever-changing state, and that Eternal Buddha's energy changes into a multiplicity of forms. That which has form changes into that which is without form, and that which is formless changes into that which has form. The term 'void' signifies this process. Consequently, it can be said that the void signifies the law of recurring movement in the universe, which consists of the processes of birth, development, decline and death.

On the other hand, 'nothingness' does not express the law

of recurring movement in the universe, because nothingness is a negation implying that nothing exists. From this standpoint, it can be said that the void is connected to time and nothingness to being.

The key to unlocking the secrets of the idea of the void is the notion of time. Actually, the idea of the void expresses the essential nature of time. The concept of time involves change, and time cannot exist in a space where there is no change, where everything has stopped and remains completely still. Time is generated only when all things change and are transformed, when they are mutable. Consequently, the idea of void is nothing other than a theory of time. Time infers the recurring process of birth, development, decline and death.

In contrast, the key to explaining the idea of nothingness is the theory of existence. What then is the nature of nothingness in relation to the theory of existence? This leads us to another question, 'How should we regard the Will that created this universe?' We tend to conceive of any existence as being solid, unmoving and stable. The idea of nothingness asks you in Zen fashion whether this way of seeing the world is in fact right. 'Does the house you live in really exist? Does the Earth really exist? Do you really exist? How about the land you stand on, the rocks, the animals?' In other words, the idea of nothingness confronts us with the question, 'If time has stopped and if there is no passage of time, is it possible that things exist?'

The idea of the void involves the passage of time, but with the idea of nothingness, time is halted; this idea asks whether the world or the whole universe can exist if time is frozen into a single moment. In light of this question, the world which people suppose solid is found to be no more than a projection of the Will of Eternal Buddha, who is the origin of all existence. In other words, the multi-layered structure of the ninth-, eighth-, seventh-, sixth-, fifth-, fourth- and third-dimensional worlds is nothing more than the projection of Buddha's Will onto the screen of each dimension, where images of landscapes and inhabitants appear, as in a movie.

Onto this screen are projected Tathagata (inhabitants of the ninth and eighth dimensions), Bodhisattva (inhabitants of the seventh dimension), the inhabitants of the sixth-dimensional Light Realm, or hell at the bottom of the fourth dimension. They are only images projected onto a screen, so as soon as the light from the projector is shut off, the images disappear. This is the explanation of how the world is structured. In fact, the idea of nothingness explains that the world is the projection of Buddha's Will, so things can suddenly come into existence and equally suddenly disappear according to His Will.

The ideas of the void and nothingness may appear to be very similar, but they are connected to a theory of time and a theory of space respectively. In other words, these are views of the world from the perspective of time (the void) and from the perspective of space or existence (nothingness).

10

A New Development in the Theory of the Void

In the context of modern society, the theory of the void will eventually merge with leading-edge physics. At present, the theories of physics seem to have come to a dead end in studies of elementary particles and the structure of the universe. What awaits modern physics beyond these boundaries are mysteries, the wonders of the spirit world. There will be no further advances in physics unless physics works hard to unravel the secrets of the mechanism and the structure of the Real World.

If we were to interpret the idea of the void in a futuristic way, it could be explained as the analysis of Buddha's Light as the source of elementary particles, also as the science of the spirit world which goes beyond Einstein's theory of relativity. Einstein's theory was based on the assumption that when the velocity of light is constant, warps occur in time and space. While Newtonian physics explained laws that were based on the premise that time and space are constant, Einstein's theory was founded on the idea that light has a constant velocity and with this as the pivot, the warping of time and space occurs; in other words, time is lengthened and shortened, and space is warped. However, Einstein's theory is about to be overturned.

There will be a discovery of 'spiritual velocity' which overrides the velocity of light, and it will become known that even the velocity of light is not constant, that it is not the ultimate criterion. Spiritual velocity is faster than the speed of light, and this is why in the spirit world it is possible to see the future. If you can travel faster than light, it is possible to see light before it is emitted by the sun. In other words, it is possible to see the world of tomorrow. Spiritual velocity will be the basis of the coming new physics. With this prediction, I would like to conclude this chapter.

[1] There is an argument that Buddhism passively adopted the idea of reincarnation from the folk beliefs of ancient India. One theory interprets Shakyamuni's teaching of egolessness in a materialistic way, and concludes that there is no such thing as a soul, so reincarnation is impossible because there is no subject to experience reincarnation. Another theory argues that there is no such thing as a soul, but that karma continues to be transmitted, just as light is passed from one candle to another.

However, it is a historical fact that Shakyamuni attained enlightenment and became an Arakan through the attainment of the three types of transcendental knowledge: 1) knowledge of one's own former lives and those of others; 2) the ability to know the future death and life of the masses; 3) the ability to get rid of delusive attachments through a knowledge of Buddha's Truth.

These three types of transcendental knowledge can be described as psychic abilities, and they clearly describe the characteristics of Shakyamuni's enlightenment. If there had been no such thing as reincarnation, it would have been impossible to penetrate past or future lives.

In his preaching, Shakyamuni actually used many stories of past lives and spoke of the possibility of attaining enlightenment in future lives. It is only natural to think that he possessed divine powers that accompanied his enlightenment. The fact that Shakyamuni possessed the transcendental power to penetrate past and future lives contributed to the evolution of the concept of reincarnation from a folk belief into Truth.

In fact, as someone who possesses the same transcendental powers as Shakyamuni, I cannot help but be surprised at the superficial and worldly interpretations of the truth of reincarnation on the part of Buddhist scholars long after Shakyamuni's passing.

CHAPTER FIVE

The Law of Causality

The Concept of the Invisible Bond Between People

In this chapter, I would like to focus on the law of causality, another important key to understanding Shakyamuni's teachings. In Japan, where there is a long tradition of Buddhism, people still tend to believe that an invisible tie exists between people and they greatly value this kind of connection. There is, for example, a popular saying that goes, 'Even the person whose shoulder you accidentally brush against has some connection to you from past lives.'

It could be said that the idea of love is behind this way of looking at human relationships; in other words, it is a way of seeing people as interconnected by invisible bonds. According to this thinking, any acquaintance, even one that seems to come about quite by chance, is in fact preordained by these invisible bonds. You may detect overtones of fatalism, but this idea of relationships arranged in heaven is meaningful because there is the willingness to find a connection with people through Buddha's providence, instead of distancing them or regarding them as total strangers.

Currently the population of the spirit world is estimated to be slightly higher than fifty billion. Of these souls a very limited number are born into one particular place and into a particular era, to create a civilization specific to the region or nation and to develop relationships with one another. Consequently, you can assume that those people you encounter, who have been born into the same era in the same place as you, are part of a very specific group of spirits. In fact, if you could see the past lives of those around you, you would find that you had had relationships in the past.

Of the numerous people you encounter in this world, one person may, for some reason, become extremely close to you; this person may become your friend, your spouse, your teacher or your student. It is difficult to regard these relationships merely as coincidence. Actually, you have had close relationships with such people in past lives, too; and past relationships, such as those of a parent and child, brother and sister, a friend and so on, are repeating themselves in a number of different forms. Of course, new relationships may be formed in this life, but even this sort of newly-formed bond is also the result of heavenly guidance, and it will develop into other different forms of relationship in future lives.

Success and failure in life have a lot to do with human relationships, which are in effect a chain of invisible bonds.

Depending on your relationships with others, your business may succeed or fail, you may get a promotion or you may not. The Buddhist concept of the invisible bond that exists between people can be explained as a theory of human relationships. It is also a form of research into love, from a new angle.

2

The Law of Cause and Effect

Following my brief illustration of the invisible bonds between people, I would like to talk about the law of cause and effect, which is also considered distinctive of Buddhism.

When you look at a couple, with the idea of the spiritual bond in mind, you can sometimes conclude that they are married because of a marriage bond in a past life. To apply this sort of perception more generally makes it clear that certain actions bring about certain effects; a good cause will bring about a good effect, and a bad cause will bring about a bad effect. These causes and effects are the workings of one of the most fundamental laws governing human life. The reason Buddhism has been successful as a philosophy as well as a religion is that it has a deep insight into this law of cause and effect.

Why would it be that the relationships we are now subject to – parent and child, brother and sister, husband and wife –

have in many cases originated in past lives? The reason is that we have enjoyed relationships with those we are now close to in the past, too. Because we felt 'we were happy together and enjoyed the relationship', be it that of husband and wife, parent and child, brother and sister, our relationships from past lives repeat.

If you think in this way, you will understand that every day you are sowing the seeds of causes. If you sow seeds every day, you will see the effects of your actions in the way the seeds sprout and grow.

It can be said that the law of cause and effect is the Buddhist philosophy of success, and also the philosophy of happiness. People often misunderstand Buddhism, believing it teaches only human suffering and focuses on the sadder side of human life, but this is wrong. Like many other great philosophers, Shakyamuni taught the philosophy of happiness, which can in fact be summarized as the law of cause and effect.

To get the fruit that is called 'happiness', you have to sow the seeds of happiness, then water them, fertilize them, and put them in the sun to help them grow. This law of cause and effect is an important part of achieving success. It is a universal rule. Each and every person can practise this law in their daily lives, and they will confirm that any wholehearted endeavour will always be rewarded in one way or another.

Of course, the effort you make may not be rewarded directly. For example, you may fail the entrance exams to a college, even though you studied extremely hard. However, your hard work can never be wasted; it will have a positive effect on your future. On the other hand, as the proverb says, 'Bad news travels fast'; if you secretly do something malicious, unintentionally it will be revealed, and eventually bring you misfortune.

If you see life as governed by rules, it can be viewed as the manifestation of a chain of cause and effect. The seeds you have sown may not bear fruit in this lifetime, but it is also true that you can never expect to see flowers unless you have first sown seeds.

To teach this truth, Shakyamuni said, 'You should not simply lament over unhappiness, which is the result of the past; instead, continue to sow seeds of happiness for the future. As a practice for doing this, did I not teach the importance of making an effort to develop yourself, giving offerings to others and conveying the Truth to many, with the intention of guiding them to happiness? These virtuous acts will bring you happiness in the end. You may not be able to reap the harvest of your efforts while you live on this Earth, but the time will come when you will receive the fruits, if not in this world then perhaps after you return to heaven. It is as if you are laying up treasure in a heavenly storehouse.' I hope you have understood that the law of cause and effect is a theory of attaining happiness within the flow of time.

What is Karma?

A discussion of the law of cause and effect will lead us to consider the idea of karma. It is often said that human beings are doomed by karma. Despite the fact that everyone is born equal, if you look at people's lives you may wonder about the differences, not only in terms of appearances but also in terms of the inner life. Where are the origins of these differences to be found? You may feel that their roots cannot necessarily be found in a present life; if human beings reincarnate eternally, the cumulative effects of past lives must exert some sort of influence.

When we look at karma, as a rule there should be both positive and negative aspects to it, but the word karma tends to have negative connotations. In the Buddhist tradition, karma is a concept that has been used to explain the reason for misfortunes one might encounter in life. For instance, if you have been hurt by someone, that may be because in a past life you hurt someone; the reason you are blind in this life may be that you damaged someone's sight in a past life; if you suffer from a handicap that affects the legs, that may be because in a past life you injured someone else's legs; you may suffer humiliation in this life because you humiliated someone in a past life; if in this life you are cursed, that may be because you cursed someone in a past life, and so on.

According to this logic, the accumulation of past wrong-doings results in karma, which has a negative influence on your present life. Much of the misfortune you experience in this life must be the reflection of others' resentment, and their negative thoughts and ill-will must be what is preventing you from achieving success. This is how people tend to perceive karma.

As the result of my own experiences reading people's past lives, I can say that events from past lives do have some bearing on this life. If a person's life is perceived as an exercise book of problems to solve, in many cases the most distinctive problems have their source not only in this life but also in past lives. However, life's difficulties should not simply be regarded fatalistically, as punishment for sins committed in past lives.

A man who committed a murder in a past life may perhaps be murdered in this life. However, this will not necessarily occur as punishment for his past crime. He may have volunteered to take the role of victim. It is true that human beings can only learn through experience, so a person may choose voluntarily to have a difficult life.

This master plan for your life does not only contain good things. It involves all the necessary steps to be followed for maximum soul growth and development. Before we come down to live an earthly life, we each draw up a life plan, fully aware of these conditions.

To put it in a more modern way, karma can be explained as the tendencies of the soul, because karma is the imprint of memories from past lives that remains in each soul. Each person has tendencies characteristic of his or her individual soul, and when situations similar to those faced in past lives recur, people therefore tend to repeat the same patterns of action and get caught in the same sorts of traps over and over again. When you think of karma as the tendencies of the soul, it is important to ask yourself, 'What are most prominent soul tendencies? Based on these tendencies, what sort of problems am I likely to encounter in my life?' The answer will differ from person to person.

I would like you to understand the word 'karma' as 'the tendencies of the soul'. When you look at your own tendencies and consider carefully what you can do about them, you will be able to live constructively.

Fatalism

This discussion of the law of cause and effect and of karma may have left some of you wondering where fatalism fits in, so let us now consider the subject of fate. We can start by examining whether or not karma and destiny are the same thing. Indeed, it is possible to say that karma is one of the elements that constitute a person's destiny.

If you are a driver, you will have noticed that each car has its own distinctive characteristics. A certain car may be fast or slow, it may be fuel-efficient whereas another is not. One model can make sharp turns better than another. One model may cause trouble when you go uphill, while another may not have very much capacity to carry things. The tendencies of the individual soul are similar. They are rather like the different characteristics of cars.

If you imagine that each person moves through the course of life as if they are driving a car, it is important to drive the car in the manner that is most appropriate, or that best suits its characteristics. If you regard destiny as the course a life takes, karma can be seen as the different levels of perform-ance of the cars as they are driven on the road of destiny, or the different characteristics of ships that go down the river of destiny. On the basis of a given situation and the tendencies of one's soul, it is possible to foresee what kind of life a person will live.

For a better understanding of this, it may help to consider what happens in tenpin bowling. If you release the ball in a certain direction with a certain amount of force, you can estimate how many pins you will be able to knock down. In a similar way it is possible to assess your own life.

You may ask the fundamental question of whether there is actually such a thing as destiny. The answer is that there are a number of factors that make up what is known as des-tiny, although in each individual case the content and extent of the influence of each factor is different. The first factor is karma, or the tendencies of the soul; the second is the family environment in which you are brought up; the third factor is the social environment and the times in which you live; the fourth is the effort you make; and the fifth is the assistance of others.

Of the five factors that are to form your destiny, the fourth, the effort you make, and the fifth, the assistance of other people, are left undecided, whereas the other ele-ments, the tendencies of your soul, your family, and the social environment of the particular era are already fixed when you are born. So it can be said that to a certain extent your destiny is already determined and unchange-able, but there is room for change in your life, depending on the effort you make and how much help you receive from others.

To conclude this section, I would like to say that your destiny is shaped according to the combination of conditions pre-determined at birth and other factors that you are able to change through your own efforts.

5

The Nature of
Free Will

In connection to the discussion of destiny, I would now like to focus on free will. If you ask whether there is such a thing as free will, the answer is yes, but the truth is that although you can exert your own will, it is also subject to restriction by external factors.

Let me use as an example a packed train at rush hour. Suppose you board the last carriage of the train, and you want to move all the way through to the front car. Is it possible to do this by the time you get to your station? It is probably impossible to elbow your way through the train. In theory, you could walk all the way, but in actual fact it is practically impossible because of the presence of all the others packing the train. On the other hand, if you want to walk through from the back to the front of the train during off-peak hours, it is quite easy to so. In the difference between these two situations is the key to solving the question about free will.

In your life you may encounter a situation that you cannot possibly change with your own will, and at other times you may be able to cut a way through, using your own will. It is important to judge which kind of situation you have been placed in. When you cannot break through with your own efforts, just as when you are in a packed train, you will never be able to move freely unless you find an alternative route.

One way of solving the problem is to wait until other people get off the train and make room. Another way may be to get out of the carriage at the back and walk along the platform towards the front car. However, the latter case completely ignores the condition that you have to be on the train, and it means that you must use your free will in a quite exceptional way. This is similar to a moment in life when something totally unexpected happens, as if you are cut off from your past and enter a totally new dimension. At this very moment, your destiny changes. If you cannot get through in the usual way, you may be able to cut through in a totally unexpected way.

Consequently, it is appropriate to think of there being two levels of free will that you can exercise to solve problems. The first level is free will within an ordinary context: if you are unable to force a situation to change, the only thing you can do is to wait. The second level is an exceptional way of exercising free will: if you cannot move inside the train, you can take decisive action and get off and walk along outside the train to get to the front.

Attaining enlightenment through the disciplines of Buddhism can be compared to the situation where a passenger who finds difficulty in moving ahead in a full train makes the decision to get off. Of course, there is a danger that he will miss the train unless he gets off fast, moves quickly and gets back on again before the doors shut. Perhaps this risk can be likened to the hardship that accompanies self-discipline on the path to enlightenment. In essence, the discipline for attaining enlightenment is a special method of fighting your way out of difficulties. It is a rather special way of exercising your free will to achieve unexpected results.

6

The Concept of Hell

If we expand our discussion of the law of causality, we will come to the concepts of heaven and hell. Buddhism explains the various realms of heaven and hell in greater detail than Christianity, and this is largely due to the fact that while living on Earth, Shakyamuni himself travelled to many different realms in the other world.

During meditation Shakyamuni would often slip out of his body and visit different regions in heaven and hell. Afterwards, he would give his disciples detailed accounts of his travels. As they continued hearing stories of the other world, gradually they were able to form a clearer picture of heaven and hell, and their belief in them deepened.

Buddhism describes the realms of hell very clearly, whereas Christianity, although it teaches that unless people believe in Christ they will go to hell, does not seem to give specific details. The reason that the Buddhist tradition describes the many different regions of hell and their inhabitants so clearly is that Shakyamuni himself was a powerful psychic. Many of his disciples, including those who lived in later years, also possessed psychic abilities which enabled them to experience the dark realm in the other world that is known as hell.

The reason for teaching the concept of hell can be summarized in the following two points.

Firstly, it was to educate. If people think that death is the ultimate conclusion of a life, they will be easily tempted by the many forms of worldly pleasure and suffer the burning pains that result from attachment. However, Buddhism teaches that life after death exists beyond a doubt, and that those who have lived their lives on Earth and had vicious thoughts and done vicious deeds will unquestionably be subject to judgement. Because these sorts of teachings aroused people's fears, they contributed to the strengthening of their faith.

Whether it be in ancient times or today, advanced souls are prepared to listen to advanced teachings, in contrast with those who are not so developed, who often will not believe or learn unless they feel threatened by the possibility of a disaster or misfortune which might affect them personally. The idea of danger can serve as an expedient measure in awakening people.

The second reason for teaching the concept of hell is to clarify the true nature of human existence. After we leave this world on Earth, the place where we will go is made up solely of thoughts. People whose minds are filled with diabolical thoughts will roam in the shapes of devils. Those whose minds are full of vengeful thoughts will turn into vengeful ghosts. This clearly illustrates just how substantial human thoughts are, and how vile thoughts give rise to a vile reality.

The Reality of Hell

Many people probably think that hell is merely imaginary, but hell is not just a thought, it is a reality. The fact that it actually exists does not necessarily mean that Eternal Buddha created it, but for those who inhabit that realm, it is a reality.

What sorts of dreams do you have when you are sick and feverish? Perhaps they are dreams of darkness, and of a cold, sad world. In your dreams, you may recall being chased by somebody who was trying to kill you, falling into a hole or having a bad accident. When you have unpleasant experiences in your dreams, it is highly likely that you are getting a glimpse of hell. You could say that hell is nothing other than a nightmare.

The good thing about a dream is that once you have awakened, it is all over. On the other hand, the nightmare of hell is not over so easily; it may take hundreds of years to awaken from the nightmare. The inhabitants of hell always say, 'It must be a dream, it must be a nightmare. A situation as terrible as this cannot be real.' Strangely enough, however, their nightmares do not go away easily because for those people it is their reality, and unless they change themselves, they cannot get out.

Heaven and hell do not exist somewhere in the invisible world. In the same way as heaven is not located high in the sky, hell is not found deep in the earth. Heaven and hell exist in the same world that we inhabit. Within this three-dimensional world, the other world exists, and people's inner worlds connect them to various parts of it.

Although not visible to human eyes, hell and heaven exist in the space where we are, on the streets where we walk, in the buildings where we work, and in the schools where we study. Although you think that you are walking on a neatly paved street, in that very place a hell may be unfolding, where people kill each other. It may sound odd, but there will be a time when dreams are no longer dreams, and when the thoughts within your mind will become real. You could think of the other world as a place where the time when you are awake and the time when you are asleep are reversed.

You may have had dreams that seem very real, and you may have experienced the feeling that you were watching the continuation of a dream you have had before. When this happens, it is likely that you are re-experiencing a previous visit to the spirit world. When you revisit the spirit world, you may see the sequel to scenes you saw on your last trip.

If you wish to know whether your heart and mind are attuned to heaven or hell, just examine what you experience in your dreams. If you often dream of sharing joy with others in a peaceful place, then you belong in heaven. If, on the other hand, you tend to experience situations in your dreams that are dark, sad and full of hardship where you cannot experience peace of mind, it means that you are visiting hell in your sleep. If this is the case, I would like you to know that this suggests where you may go after you die.

When the dream is no longer a dream but becomes a reality, what will you do? In this situation, the only thing you can rely on is your knowledge of Buddha's Truth. Whether you have studied or not will make the crucial difference. If you study Buddha's Truth deeply while you live on Earth, you will know how to escape from the nightmare of hell. On the other hand, those who have not studied Truth will have absolutely no idea what to do, and in hell there will be no school to teach you. As the famous saying goes, 'Knowledge is power.'

8

The Concept of Heaven

Following our exploration of hell, let us look at the Buddhist concept of heaven. The Buddhist heaven is roughly divided into three regions. First, there is the realm of human beings where good-natured people go. Second, there is the realm of heaven, where those who are highly advanced in their discipline and radiance go. Above that exists the realm of Buddha, inhabited by Buddha and the gods. This is a picture of the Buddhist heaven.

From my observation, though, the world that is known as heaven is divided into many different levels, according to the attributes of the inhabitants. It is a very intricate structure composed of carefully segmented realms. Although I use the names fourth, fifth, sixth, seventh, eighth and ninth dimensions to explain the other world, each dimension is actually divided into smaller parts. The other world is composed of consciousness or thoughts, so even a slight difference in the level of consciousness of inhabitants will cause them to live separately. As a result, 'heaven' consists of many different realms.

However, it is true that the world known as heaven can be roughly divided into several levels: the Realm of the Good (fifth dimension), where the inhabitants have awakened to human goodness; the Light Realm (sixth dimension), whose inhabitants have achieved success on Earth while at the same time possessing an inner quality of goodness; and above these the Bodhisattva Realm (seventh dimension) and the Tathagata Realm (eighth dimension) where the highly evolved spirits or angels live.

Buddhism states explicitly that the realm of high spirits or angels exists, and that these angels are engaged in many different sorts of work. Describing the different occupations of the angels is a characteristic of Buddhism. The other world is connected to this world, and those who live in this world will eventually return to the other world so it cannot be completely beyond the imagination of people here in this world on Earth. Just as each and every person on Earth has work to do, so too the inhabitants of the other world are occupied fulfilling their own tasks.

The Reality of Heaven

What is heaven really like? How would you feel if you were actually there? Heaven is usually said to be filled with brilliant light. It is sometimes called the world of perpetual bliss, or everlasting summer. It could be called the world of joy. If I were to describe it in an earthly way, I would say heaven is like a place where close friends get together and enjoy talking with one another.

The most distinctive characteristic of the inhabitants of heaven is, in a word, innocence. They are artless and pure. They have hearts of gold, the basic requirement for living in heaven. The inhabitants of heaven are always willing to be gentle to others and at the same time willing to do what is truly good for themselves. They do good because of a desire to spread happiness around them, rather than causing others harm.

If I were to make a summary of the minimum requirements for living in heaven, one would be that you are able to live always with a smile on your face, not a superficial smile but a natural smile. The inhabitants of heaven live like this. So, when you practise self-reflection, if you cannot determine what it is that you must correct, I would like to suggest that you do a simple mental exercise; imagine that you have no social status, position or reputation that you can rely on, and then decide honestly whether you would still have a natural smile on your face.

Another point to consider is that no one in heaven was disliked by others when living on Earth. This may sound simplistic, but it is quite true that heaven is a place where people that others like live. Those people who are liked by others are actually the ones who have liked others. It is a rule that people who like others are also liked by them.

So, if you wish to return to heaven, you have to be someone who is sincere, and who always has a smile on their face, who gives love to many and is liked by many. If you cannot satisfy these simple requirements, the door of heaven will not open for you.

Those who boast about their shrewdness, who are smug and self-satisfied while causing others to resent them, must stop for a moment and think. Where do those that others hate go? 'To be liked by others' does not mean craving love from others. What I am attempting to say is that those whose presence makes others uncomfortable cannot live in heaven. Heaven is a place where everything you think is transparent, it is as if others can see through your mind. So if you entertain evil thoughts you cannot live there in harmony with others as if you are a part of a flock of sheep grazing peacefully together. One way of describing the reality of heaven is that it is a place inhabited by those who feel no shame in exposing what they think. Those whose minds are full of vile thoughts, thoughts that are odorous and evil, will not be allowed to live in heaven because of the bad smell.

I would like you to reflect deeply on whether you can expose what you think publicly, without hesitation or shame. If you feel you have to hide this or that, you should know that heaven is still far from your reach.

For a human being the ideal life is to live appreciated and thought highly of by both others and yourself, while living candidly, innocently and simply. Living in heaven is no more difficult than that. First, it is essential to live the kind of life that both you and others can celebrate, then, as the next stage, those who are able to exert a greater influence will be commissioned to do grander tasks as angels.

The Principle for Establishing the World of the Eternal Buddha

In this chapter, I have explored fatalism, free will and heaven and hell, starting from a discussion of the law of causality. The reason Buddhism teaches the concept of heaven and hell is that the daily work of each person sowing seeds for the future will eventually contribute to the creation of heaven or hell. So, to attain the goal of creating a Buddha Land, in other words, a utopia on Earth where all people live together in harmony and fulfilment, we need to lead a heavenly life while still living in this world on Earth.

What kind of seeds do we need to sow for this? First, it is necessary to have a deep understanding of the law of causality, and based on this understanding we need to aim to live in a way that will not harm others or ourselves, a way of living that will enhance our happiness and add to the happiness of others.

People may say that a good person is always the one who loses out, and that an honest person is the one who makes a fool of himself. Nevertheless, you may as well be good, you may as well be honest. An honest person may sometimes appear naïve, but artless, trusting and wholehearted living itself contributes to the creation of utopia on Earth. It is important to live sincerely. Live honestly. Live a life that will bring no one any harm and at the same time believe that everything is in a process of purification and development. Live the life of an angel.

Creating utopia on Earth is not an easy task but it will become possible when each and every person understands the law of causality. Life consists of chains of cause and effect, so if you do not forget to create good causes, you will in time be surrounded by good effects. Even if you are surrounded by unpleasant occurrences and unfavourable situations, those are merely the fruits of seeds you have sown in the past. What you should do now, at this moment, is to concentrate on sowing good seeds for the future. This is the very essence of a philosophy of positive thinking and it allows you to live a life filled with light. In reality, to practise the spirit of this philosophy requires a deep understanding of the law of causality, because the situation you are now facing may be the harvest of tares sown earlier, but if you concentrate on sowing seeds of good wheat from this point on, you can expect a good harvest. If you continue to hold to this philosophy, the world that surrounds you will start to shine with a golden light. I would like you to live every day of your life in this way.

CHAPTER SIX

The Philosophy of Human Perfection

What is
Enlightenment?

In this final chapter, I would like to explore 'enlighten-ment', a subject that is at once old and new. It can be said that the attraction of Buddhism stems mainly from Shakyamuni's teachings of enlightenment for individuals. Enlightenment is a most interesting concept. It is reminiscent of a human being standing with both feet firmly on the ground who intends to develop through his own strength, not a helpless being who can be saved only by the mercy of an outside power. This must be one of the secrets of Buddhism's popularity.

At its very base, Buddhism embraces strong power. Some misunderstand it to be a pessimistic teaching for the weak but, in actual fact, Buddhism includes a methodology for becoming strong and independent. In Shakyamuni's time, two thousand five hundred years ago, this teaching that each and every individual could attain enlightenment and become a buddha, or an awakened one, was truly epoch-making. Some may argue that this idea came out of the Great Vehicle (Mahayana) schools in later years, but its source can in fact be traced back to the time when Gautama delivered his first sermon to the five seekers, who as a result attained an Arhat-level enlightenment.

We can live for the sake of others, for society or our country, but it is impossible to forget ourselves completely. All human thought tends to begin and end with the 'self', so any ideology or theory that neglects the individual 'self' will not bear fruit. In communist countries, for instance, where the highest good was to work for the sake of the state, people eventually lost their motivation to work and their desire to improve themselves.

This subject is connected to the question of how we perceive the individual in relation to the whole. Individual souls were created through a splitting off from the life form of Eternal Buddha. Originally each soul was a part of the whole, and the reason individual souls exist separately is that each one is expected to develop its own character fully and to shine with its own unique light.

Ultimately it is desirable that humanity as a whole develops, but inevitably we have to start by refining our own individual character. It is impossible to treat people as a mass, without distinguishing people one from another. Each person was originally one particle of Buddha's Light, Light which scattered and came to have its own individuality, so it is important that each particle of light shines with its own unique brilliance.

The concept of enlightenment is not only connected to the salvation of the individual soul, it also involves strong, positive qualities, values that people live for. Enlightenment is the answer to the question, 'How can I, born into such a transient world on Earth, find a reason for living, a reason for being here?' In other words, enlightenment is the heightening of our awareness, an understanding of the objective and mission of our own lives, and knowledge of the secrets of the universe. Ultimately, enlightenment is 'understanding' in the truest sense, and this gives us a great sense of happiness and strength.

I would like you to understand that enlightenment is not a limited concept aiming only at development of the individual; rather, it implies that each individual shines with a unique light.

2

Prerequisites for Enlightenment

What are the prerequisites for attaining enlightenment? What do we have to think about, in terms of preparing ourselves to become enlightened? There are three pre-conditions.

Firstly, it is necessary to recognize that human beings have infinite potential. Without this, enlightenment would lose all meaning at the outset. If a human being is defined as a weak, pitiful thing to be tossed about by the torrents of the river of destiny, there can be no possibility of enlightenment, but Buddhism recognizes the infinite goodness of human nature.

Secondly, it should be remembered that if you do not aspire to enlightenment, there is no hope of attaining it. Unless you first desire it, you cannot attain enlightenment. The desire to improve yourself does not come from outside, so unless there is a strong desire for advancement that springs from within, you cannot possibly attain enlightenment. Awakening to an aspiration for enlightenment is vital; it is both your obligation and right.

Thirdly, it is necessary to understand that human beings can achieve results through their efforts. This means that if you sow the seeds, you will reap the fruit, as I explained in the previous chapter. Unless you accept this truth, there can be no possibility of attaining enlightenment. If you make an effort, you can expect a fitting reward: you need to understand this law of cause and effect.

In this world, your efforts may not always be tangibly rewarded. In the world of the mind, however, if you sow a seed, it will unfailingly bear fruit. In this world, if you do something for somebody out of good intentions, your efforts may not always bear fruit. In fact, at times you may even be misunderstood. On the other hand, in the spirit world, if you conceive a kind thought and express it in an action, the result is already there. You can be certain that in the spirit world there are no exceptions to the law of cause and effect.

To conclude this section, let me summarize the three prerequisites for attaining enlightenment: 1) believing in the unlimited potential of human beings; 2) taking the initiative in aspiring to enlightenment and stepping forward courageously; 3) believing that in the world of enlightenment the law of cause and effect is 100 per cent certain. If you sow seeds and make the effort to encourage them to grow, they cannot fail to bear fruit.

The Methodology for Attaining Enlightenment

What kind of methods are available for attaining enlightenment? Are there any specific ways of working toward this goal? To answer these questions, I would like to suggest the following three options.

The first option is to devote all your time to self-discipline, with the aim of acquiring spiritual wisdom and increasing your level of understanding, in some cases through experiencing spiritual phenomena. This is the path of wholly devoted seekers and professional religious leaders.

'Devote all your time to the study of Buddha's Truth, and every day put your study into practice. Seek opportunities to be in contact with the spiritual realm, and through this you can deepen your understanding. Then observe the world and also yourself on the basis of this spiritual perspective.'

This has been and still is an authentic method of attaining enlightenment.

One of the outstanding characteristics of Shakyamuni's order was that it could produce expert religious leaders, people who could be called 'professionals'. Perhaps partly because society then was not as complex as it is today, many people did not hesitate to abandon their secular lives to pursue the path to enlightenment. Abandoning the secular life meant that a person was determined to live the life of a full-time seeker of enlightenment.

There may be some argument about whether it is actually necessary to abandon the secular life but it is always true that if you wish to become an expert in any walk of life and accomplish something meaningful in the world, you must devote yourself wholeheartedly to your goal. Anyone wanting to be an accomplished actor must put a great deal of energy into developing the skills of acting. No artist would be able to paint a picture that could touch people's hearts unless he or she had continued painting hundreds of pieces to achieve the expert skills. A Sunday painter will never make a true artist. In accord with this universal truth, Shakyamuni put a lot of emphasis on creating expert religious leaders through education and training within his order.

The second option is discipline for lay seekers. The idea is that while remaining firmly based in the secular world and living a worldly life, the mind is set free in the world of Buddha's Truth and spare time is devoted to exploration, study and the spread of Buddha's Truth. I think that this second option for attaining enlightenment is very important if the

Truth is to be conveyed widely. It is not possible for most people to devote all their efforts to the path of Buddha's Truth and become full-time seekers, so the method of discipline for lay seekers is very important.

As opposed to the discipline of 'professional' seekers, that of lay seekers is more difficult in a sense, as their daily lives are often lived out in environments that are a long way from the world of Truth. It could be said that lay seekers are handicapped compared to full-time seekers. It is as if they are running on sandy ground with weights in their shoes.

On the other hand, however, constantly setting your mind to explore Buddha's Truth and living as a seeker in the midst of adverse circumstances will be an excellent training that strengthens you. In this sense, lay seekers are in an advantageous position to refine their souls.

The third option for attaining enlightenment is to interpret enlightenment in many different ways and let it infiltrate into many different fields in the world. In contrast to the second method of attaining enlightenment, which draws a clear line between undertakings in the secular life and the discipline on the path of Buddha's Truth, this third option means emancipating enlightenment from the religious world and bringing it into the secular world. To do this, you are expected not only to seek enlightenment but also to share your understanding with others, transforming it into different forms. This is applying your knowledge of Buddha's Truth to a wide range of fields: to art, literature, philosophy, to business problems and to situations you come across in family life.

This third option veers away a little from the main path to enlightenment, but it is a method of attaining enlightenment for those who know their own limitations and do their best to put their learning into practice. This is not the way of the 'professional' seeker, but an applied form of self-discipline for the lay seeker. It is a method of attaining enlightenment through the practice of putting the knowledge of Buddha's Truth into action in one's daily life.

4

The Mechanism of Enlightenment

Next, I would like to explore the mechanism of enlightenment, but first I need to clarify the structure and workings of the soul and the mind. Let me begin by defining 'soul' and 'mind.'

First of all, what I call the 'soul' is a spiritual energy form of exactly the same shape as the physical body and enveloped within it. With my spiritual sight, I can see the soul enclosed in a person's body, and it is of exactly the same size, complete with eyes, nose, mouth and other features. A soul is essentially a formless entity, but when it dwells within the physical body it takes a life-sized form.

On the other hand, what I call the 'mind' is the central core of the soul. The mind could be likened to the yolk of an egg. It is the control centre of the soul and, described visually, it is situated close to the physical heart. Each soul is connected to the world of infinity through its core, the mind. Although individual souls exist separately, the part called the 'mind' is connected to the infinite world. With spiritual eyes, the part of the human mind that is connected to the infinite world sometimes looks like a rope, or rather a tube. If you trace a path through the tube, it leads to many different realms in the spirit world. While a human soul exists in the third-dimensional world, enveloped in the physical body, its core called the mind is connected to spiritual realms that range from the fourth dimension to the ninth.

This must sound rather strange to you. You may feel it is quite beyond your imagination, but it is important to know about the structure of the world of the mind. This awareness is reminiscent of the philosophical concept of 'One is many, and many are one.' Something exists and is at the same time non-existent; something is non-existent and yet exists. The world of the mind is where things that appear to contradict one another can exist compatibly.

If you could look through the 'window' that is your mind, what you would see on the other side is nothing other than the Real World. It looks as if you are gazing at the world through a telescope in an observatory on top of a high-rise building. If you bring it into focus, you can get a close-up view of busy city streets, and you can see mountains in the distance as well. In the same way that you control a lens, you can see many different worlds depending on the distance at which you set the focus of your mind. In fact, it could be said that enlightenment is a method of controlling the focus of your mind.

The mechanism of enlightenment is related to the existence of different dimensions in the multi-layered structure of the Real World. The level of your enlightenment can be determined by the direction, the degree of magnification, and the focal length with which you look at objects through the telescope of your mind. From where you are, you can choose to look either close up or into the distance. The choice is entirely up to you. I talk about the many different realms of the Real World, but these are not places far away from where you are. You can perceive and actually experience them at this very moment.

The Effects of Enlightenment

I have described the attainment of enlightenment as the equivalent of controlling the focus of a telescope to view objects that are at different distances. What then would the effect of enlightenment be? What would enlightenment bring you? What sort of benefits can you expect through attaining enlightenment? These may be the questions in your mind now. I would like to summarize the effects of enlightenment in these three points.

Firstly, as your understanding improves, you will be able to eliminate your worries, suffering and anxieties of a worldly nature.

Secondly, as a result of attaining enlightenment, you will be able to benefit a greater number of people. The better you come to know yourself and the world, the more effectively you will know how to help people become truly happy and develop themselves. Enlightenment works to refine the character and increases the influence you have on others, which will benefit more and more people around you.

The third effect of attaining enlightenment is born of enlightenment itself, and it is a feeling of true happiness. This is a feeling completely different from any sense of worldly happiness, for instance, that arises with an increase in salary, a promotion or when others praised you. True happiness of awakening to Buddha's Truth is the greatest pleasure the human spirit can experience. Without having experienced this supreme bliss, you cannot claim you are living a true life. Enlightenment is the greatest gift that Eternal Buddha has granted human beings living on this Earth. Without having known this happiness, you do not deserve to be called truly human.

To summarize, there are mainly three effects you can expect from attaining enlightenment: 1) with a higher level of understanding you can eliminate your sufferings; 2) your ability to benefit other people increases; 3) you can savour the supreme bliss that accompanies enlightenment itself.

6

What is the Arhat State?

In Shakyamuni's teaching, the most important educational objective was to attain the Arhat state. The reason that so much importance was placed on this state is that it is the first level to aim for when you are walking the path to human perfection, and that it is also a state that allows communication with high spirits in the other world. In other words, the Arhat state is the first stage where you can begin to perceive the existence of the Real World, and live as if you were in the Real World while still in this world.

According to the multi-layered structure of the spirit world that I teach, the Arhat state is equivalent to an enlightenment of the upper divisions of the sixth-dimensional Light Realm. The sixth-dimensional enlightenment is the stage at which you attain enlightenment mainly through an intellectual study of Buddha's Truth. If you are in the upper levels of that dimension, it means you are preparing to proceed to the next level, the Bodhisattva Realm of the seventh dimension. In other words, the Arhat state is the gateway to the Bodhisattva Realm.

Strictly speaking, the Arhat state can be broken down into several levels, but here I am dividing it into roughly two categories. The first stage is called 'Arhat-in-progress', which means you are moving forward on the way to attaining the Arhat state. The second stage is called the 'fruit-of-Arhat', where you have already attained Arhat state.

What is the difference between Arhat-in-progress and the fruit-of-Arhat? If you are wholeheartedly devoted to living the life of a seeker, while being free from worries and sufferings, if you are constantly making an effort to advance on the path of Truth, it can be said that you are at the 'Arhat-in-progress' stage. On the other hand, to become a fruit-of-Arhat, you have to maintain this state for at least two or three years. If you can successfully sustain a state of mind that is calm and free from attachment for three years, it can be said that you have reached the stage of the fruit-of-Arhat. During this period, you may encounter some situations that disturb the mind, but you have to be able to weather this inner turbulence. You also need to practise self-reflection regularly, to continue in your discipline on the path of Truth, and you have to be capable of receiving guidance from the heavenly realm. Unless you manage to sustain this state of mind for several years, you cannot claim to be 'fruit-of-Arhat'.

In certain exceptional cases, it is possible for people to

become Arhat-in-progress in a matter of days or in a week. If they can recall all memories since they were small, reflect upon wrong thoughts and deeds from the past one by one, and allow tears of repentance ('the rain of Dharma') to stream down their cheeks, they may hear the voices of their own guardian spirits and be bathed in the Light of their guardian spirit, and as a result reach the Arhat state.

Although some may reach the Arhat-in-progress state very quickly, the question is whether or not this condition can be sustained. A one-week course on reflective meditation in a remote mountain retreat may allow you to reach a state close to that of Arhat. However, as soon as you return to ordinary life, impurities that overshadow your mind will start to collect once again. Only if you are able to hold for two or three years to the pledge of a new beginning that you make after shedding tears of repentance, can you attain the state of fruit-of-Arhat. If you are to leave this world in this state of mind, you will certainly return to the world of Arhat in the upper reaches of the sixth-dimensional Light Realm.

Unfortunately, I have to tell you that many of those who have managed to reach the Arhat-in-progress state fall back, like climbers just about to reach the summit of a mountain but who start to lose their hold and tumble down the slope. The possibility of attaining the Arhat-in-progress state is open to everyone; 100 per cent of those who study Buddha's Truth diligently and continue their self-discipline can achieve this. In contrast, reaching the level of fruit-of-Arhat is not easy; only four or five out of a hundred will be successful.

177

Furthermore, of those who attain the fruit-of-Arhat state, less than 10 per cent will qualify to proceed to the world of Bodhisattva. I have said that to become a fruit-of-Arhat, it is necessary to sustain the Arhat state for three years. Then, if you wish to become a Bodhisattva, you have to maintain the Arhat state right through your life. A prerequisite to becoming a Bodhisattva is to devote your entire life to the service of others, and this is tantamount to sustaining the state of fruit-of-Arhat for a lifetime. To become a Bodhisattva is quite difficult; if a thousand people devote themselves to discipline, only a few will attain the enlightenment of Bodhisattva.

The Discipline of
an Arhat

In this section, I would like to talk about the discipline of an Arhat. When one thousand seekers devote themselves to spiritual discipline, if they are diligent and guided by good teachers, all of them will be able to reach the state of Arhat-in-progress, and they will manage to sustain this condition for a week or two. However, only about fifty of these one thousand aspirants will make it all the way and become fruit-of-Arhat. Furthermore, only about five out of those fifty will qualify to become Bodhisattva. This difficult challenge awaits seekers of Truth.

What are the most important attitudes for Arhat, as they progress in their discipline? There are two points to remember.

Firstly, it is essential to be willing to continue in the discipline of refining yourself throughout your lifetime, until the moment you die. The human mind quickly collects impurities, just as the surface of a mirror gathers dust and becomes cloudy and dull, so it is important for you to keep on refining yourself, and to establish this habit as a part of your daily practice, like polishing a mirror. Just as you do the dishes, wash your clothes and clean your house every day, every day refine your own mind. Continue to do this for the rest of your life.

Secondly, humility is important because the greatest danger for Arhat is conceit. Seekers who have reached the Arhat state tend to be easily satisfied with a low level of enlightenment and a low level of success. This is the level at which seekers may start to experience spiritual phenomena such as seeing the auras of others or hearing the voices of their own guardian spirits. As a result, some seekers may make the mistake of judging themselves to be great Bodhisattva of Light.

In the Arhat state, it is absolutely necessary for you to reflect on yourself with humility. If you do ever experience spiritual phenomena, do not become conceited but accept this calmly as an experience, and have the wisdom to know the gem in a pile of rocks. Stability is vital for spiritual perception, too. If you can take complete control of spiritual phenomena, like an expert driver who can manoeuvre a car at will, there will be no problem, but in reality most people are not capable of this.

So, the two most important attitudes to remember as you undergo the discipline of an Arhat are: 1) never forget to continue refining yourself throughout your life; 2) keep reminding yourself of the importance of humility, and be especially cautious about experiences of spiritual phenomena, because they tend to cause people to forget humility and lead them astray.

8

The Essential Nature of Bodhisattva

Following our exploration of the Arhat state, let us proceed to the next level, the Bodhisattva state. According to the rules of the spirit world, unless you reincarnate three times while maintaining the Arhat state, you cannot advance to the Bodhisattva Realm.

Although human beings repeat cycles of reincarnation many, many times, in almost all cases the only time they can reach the Arhat state while on Earth is when a great teacher has incarnated into this world. If you lead an ordinary life when there is no great teacher to guide you, it is extremely hard to attain an enlightenment of Arhat through your own efforts alone. There may be some exceptional people who succeed, as a result of the lessons they learn from experience, but the probability of this is quite low.

The time when a great number of new Arhat are born is only when a great spiritual teacher lives on Earth. For this reason, when such a teacher is expected to descend to Earth, spirits compete with one another to incarnate. If they study the Law of Truth under the guidance of the great teacher, and successfully attain the state of Arhat, this achievement will be kept as their track record. In baseball, batters are rated by their batting average once they have established a decent average, which does not fall so easily. In the same way, once you have attained the enlightenment of Arhat under a great teacher, and if you can live your next two lives in Arhat state – in other words, three lives in a row – you will then be allowed to proceed to the next stage, Bodhisattva. This is usually what happens.

As you can see, the requirements for qualification as a Bodhisattva are very strict, and you have to prove yourself over a long period of time. If the average person reincarnates once every three hundred years, it will take almost a thousand years to become a Bodhisattva after you have reached the Arhat state. Seekers who aspire to become Bodhisattva have to have a strong determination to continue in their efforts to advance on the path for a thousand years. Unfortunately, most people are likely to give up within a few years, so unless you are gifted with exceptional will power, humility and perseverance, the goal will not be reached. Nevertheless, it is also true that once you have become a Bodhisattva after a thousand years of discipline, this state of mind will not deteriorate easily.

The Bodhisattva Realm and the realms above are the domains of 'professional' teachers and educators. The gap between the professional and the amateur is not easy to bridge, so unless you refine yourself intensively and thoroughly, you will not deserve the title of 'professional'. I would like you to remember that to become a Bodhisattva requires strict self-discipline over a long period of time, and that this cannot be achieved instantly. You must not get the wrong idea that you can become a Bodhisattva simply by being kind to somebody or making a donation to a charity. It demands tremendous perseverance to continue walking the path of progress.

Altruism and love are part of the essential nature of Bodhisattva, but this love is backed by the strength unique to those who have long devoted themselves to making this world a better place to live and who have continued in their efforts to realize this goal with unyielding determination. These people are characterized by perseverance and steadfastness. Those who have steadfastly walked the narrow path holding to the goal of saving others, bringing a light to the world and creating a utopia on Earth, are fulfilling their mission as Bodhisattva.

The light that Bodhisattva give out is not a superficial glitter. It is a subdued light that shines forth from within, the fruit of their tireless discipline over hundreds and thousands of years.

The Essential Nature of Tathagata

I have said that out of one thousand Arhat-in-progress, barely five will manage to attain the enlightenment of Bodhisattva, and that it will take them a thousand years of self-discipline. Then the next question will be, 'How can a Bodhisattva become a Tathagata?' The answer is, 'They must have reincarnated twenty to thirty times while maintaining the Bodhisattva state, in different ages and regions. Only if they manage to fulfil 80 to 90 per cent of their mission each time, regardless of the region or epoch, will they be appointed Tathagata on the basis of their stable records and the outstanding abilities they have demonstrated. This means that it takes more than ten thousand years of continued success for a Bodhisattva to become a Tathagata, on condition that a Bodhisattva can maintain the state of the upper-level Bodhisattva all those years. This is an incredibly high hurdle.

Even though Bodhisattva have evolved to reach the

upper levels within the Bodhisattva Realm, they often experience ups and downs in the course of ten thousand years of reincarnations. At times, they may make mistakes. Although Bodhisattva are expected to devote themselves to altruism and guiding people, they may be misled by evil forces and believe themselves to be as exalted as primordial gods and found their own religions. The possibility of this kind of risk always remains. However, having originally been high spirits, they will eventually correct their own mistakes and come back onto the right track. In cases like this, the discipline on the path to become a Tathagata will have to start all over again. Although they may have successfully continued discipline as upper-level Bodhisattva for several thousand years, if they go astray and spend two or three hundred years correcting their mistakes, the years before that will count for nothing and they will have to start all over again.

As I have stated, the condition for becoming a Tathagata is ten thousand years of success as upper-level Bodhisattva. If a Bodhisattva fails after nine thousand years of glory, all these years are wasted and he or she will have to start out anew on another ten thousand years. As this discipline is so demanding, only one out of five hundred upper-level Bodhisattva will be successful in reaching the state of Tathagata, after ten thousand years of devotion to strenuous discipline.

According to my observations, there are about two thousand spirits at the highest level of the Bodhisattva Realm who are undergoing discipline to proceed to the Tathagata Realm. If we apply the ratio of 500:1, four out of the two thousand will successfully become Tathagata. If only four Tathagata are born every ten thousand years, it can be said that on average we can only see the birth of a new Tathagata every two thousand five hundred years. Given the fact that there are six billion people on Earth and fifty billion in total when we include the population of the spirit world, the diligent discipline of all fifty billion people produces only one Tathagata every two thousand five hundred years. A Tathagata is thus a very rare occurrence.

Nevertheless, because a new Tathagata is born only once every two thousand five hundred years, that birth will be celebrated as the greatest joy for all humankind. The birth of a Tathagata that occurs every few millennia is accompanied by an enormous light. The Real World becomes brilliantly illuminated as if a huge chandelier has been lit. When this happens, the heavenly world is filled with joy at receiving an additional force.

In the heavenly world, a strenuous effort is made constantly and steadfastly. One who has become a Tathagata is a source of spiritual energy that nourishes many, many people, like the queen bee that lays innumerable eggs. The birth of a Tathagata means the birth of a great new leader, who will guide many with his unshakeable state and superior abilities which have been developed over ten thousand years of hard work.

The total number of Tathagata in heaven is estimated to be less than five hundred. When you consider that such a small number are guiding nearly fifty billion spirits in total, each Tathagata has to be capable of leading as many as one hundred million people. This is the very reason why ten thousand years of success are required for an upper-level Bodhisattva to become Tathagata; this amount of time is needed to develop outstanding abilities of leadership necessary to guide such large numbers of people. On the other hand, it is also true that the possibility of becoming Tathagata is open to anyone who satisfies this requirement.

CANADIAN TIRE

LA SOCIÉTÉ CANADIAN TIRE LIMITÉE

CASH BONUS · BILLET · BONI

CANADIAN TIRE CORPORATION, LIMITED

Executive Vice-President and Chief Financial Officer
Vice-président directeur et chef aux finances

President and Chief Executive Officer
Président et chef de l'administration

REDEEMABLE IN MERCHANDISE ONLY AT CANADIAN TIRE STORES
REMBOURSABLE EN MARCHANDISE UNIQUEMENT AUX MAGASINS CANADIAN TIRE

5¢

REDEEMABLE IN MERCHANDISE ONLY AT CANADIAN TIRE STORES

0274892621

0274892621

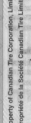

Property of Canadian Tire Corporation, Limited.
Propriété de la Société Canadian Tire Limitée.

Cash bonus coupons are redeemable in merchandise only at Canadian Tire associate stores and only in association with consumer purchases of merchandise or service in the ordinary course of retail business.

Les billets-bonis sont remboursables en merchandise uniquement aux magasins associés Canadian Tire, et cela seulement dans le cadre d'achats de marchandises ou de service, faits par un consommateur dans le cours normal des opérations de vente au détail.

REMBOURSABLE EN MARCHANDISE UNIQUEMENT AUX MAGASINS CANADIAN TIRE

The Path to Becoming a Buddha

I have said that an ordinary soul can attain the Tathagata state if it tirelessly continues in its efforts. In actual fact, there are quite a number of people who have successfully evolved to Tathagata after having started their lives as spirits created on planet Earth.

Above the Tathagata Realm is the realm of Buddhas, those who are truly awakened and enlightened, and who reign as the saviours of the planet. In our terrestrial spirit group there are ten Buddhas. A being called Buddha has an incomparable ability to take charge of an entire spirit group belonging to a planet. Can you imagine how much effort it requires for a Tathagata to become a Buddha or a Grand Tathagata of the ninth dimension? It requires a successful record as a Tathagata for at least one hundred million years. Only if he has been successful in guiding humankind for more than one hundred million years, through all his reincarnations as Tathagata, will he be allowed to enter the ninth-dimensional world of Grand Tathagata, the world of saviours. In comparison to the ten thousand years of discipline that is required before an upper-level Bodhisattva can evolve into a Tathagata, it can take as long as one hundred million years for a Tathagata to become a Grand Tathagata.

Those Tathagata in the eighth dimension, who number nearly five hundred, will have to experience one hundred million years of success to evolve into Grand Tathagata, and even a single failure during this period will bring all their previous efforts to naught and they will have to start the whole process again from nothing.

In theory, one Grand Tathagata is born every one or two hundred million years. In the terrestrial spirit group, however, there is no Grand Tathagata of Earth origin; all of the ten Grand Tathagata of our planet have originally come from other planets and have since been in charge of creating our terrestrial spirit group. In the upper area of the eighth dimension that is also called the Sun Realm, there are several high spirits who have the potential to evolve into Grand Tathagata. Perhaps the birth of a new Grand Tathagata will occur in the next few tens of millions of years.

When a new Grand Tathagata is born it is possible that the total number of ninth-dimensional Great Guiding Spirits will increase, or that one of those who is already a Grand Tathagata will leave for another planet to guide its inhabitants.

As we have seen, the human soul is in the process of eternal progress through eternal effort. The only method of attaining the ultimate victory is perseverance to continue making an effort. This attitude is to be celebrated because it will bring happiness to many. You must remember that the greatest human happiness is to bring happiness to many.

Afterword

You may have let out a sigh on reading the last chapter of this book, as you were reminded of how difficult it can be to attain enlightenment. The path to enlightenment is hard and demanding but it is your own determination that will take you to the starting line and that will be the driving force to carry you to the ultimate goal.

If this book in any way serves as a guide for your eternal spiritual evolution, the author's joy will be beyond measure.

August 1988 (for Japanese edition)
Ryuho Okawa

UNCONDITIONAL LOVE

Ed and Deb Shapiro

In the last ten years we have witnessed a massive rise in self-help and development books reflecting a growing desire to be happier and more personally fulfilled. But too often these provide only quick-fix solutions that give some clarity and direction but fail to offer a more transformative result.

Unconditional Love offers us an in-depth understanding of what it is to live in the complexity of modern life while maintaining a tender and caring heart. It is both practical and inspiring, presenting the wisdom of the East and the paths of Buddhism and Yoga in an accessible form with meditations and stories. Ed and Deb Shapiro specialise in making the ancient truths accessible and applicable to everyday life and, more specifically, in reaching those who are seeking a spiritual direction free of religious doctrine.

True happiness can only be attained through a connection to our spiritual heart. *Unconditional Love* asks that we look into ourselves and go beyond the ego to find deeper levels of loving kindness, forgiveness and tolerance. Uplifting and inspiring, it compels the reader to live with integrity, fearlessness and the vastness of an awakened heart.

'*Unconditional Love* focuses on the need for greater compassion and open-heartedness in the world. At a time when our world is increasingly interdependent and yet the future seems so uncertain . . . this is invaluable'
His Holiness The Dalai Lama

HEALING BEYOND THE BODY

Larry Dossey M.D.

'If modern medicine is to be a healing art, it must embrace three ideas it has too long ignored. It must address not only our bodies, but our minds and spirits as well; it must deal not only with the mechanism of illness, but with its meaning; and it must recognise that our power to heal and be healed extends beyond our physical bodies.'

Best-selling author of *Healing Words: The Power of Prayer* and *The Practice of Medicine*, Dr Larry Dossey is one of the most influential spokespersons for the role of consciousness and spirituality in medicine. In these writings, he explores the relationship – often documented in extensive research – between science and 'unscientific' topics such as prayer, love, laughter, work, war, creativity, dreams, and immortality.

Does the mind produce consciousness – or transmit it? Can machines detect love? Why has job stress become a worldwide epidemic? Why do objects sometimes seem to have minds of their own? Could war be a biological condition? Why is fishing good for your health? How can science study the effects of prayer? Why did Apaches believe that only when we learned to laugh were we fit to live? Dossey tackles all these questions and more. Some essays are funny, some sober, some inspirational. Each in its own way challenges us to examine ourselves and our health in a new and different light.

TAKING ADVANTAGE OF ADVERSITY

Dr Gail Feldman

'As we learn to accept change and growth cycles as
a simple fact of life, we not only become more resilient,
we also become more creative' Dr Gail Feldman

In *Taking Advantage of Adversity* Dr Gail Feldman's powerful
message is that it is possible to transform the energy
focused on major life crises into creative self-expression
and transcendent living.

In this truly inspiring book Dr Feldman casts tragedy in a
whole new light by presenting grief as a potential catalyst
for greater creativity. Using portraits of a wide range
of historical figures as examples, plus clinical case studies,
she successfully illustrates how pain and depression can
be transformed into powerful self-expression.

Her pioneering work in this field provides a map
for finding possibility and creativity among the ruins
of personal loss and life change. This is no less than
alchemy of the spirit.

TOTAL I CHING

Stephen Karcher

The I Ching is the oldest and most respected oracle
or divinatory system in the world. It has helped people for
2500 years to connect to the Way or Tao and experience
their helping spirit. There are currently two kinds of
translations available which offer somewhat conflicting
interpretations – the popular Confucian version and an
earlier version called Zhouyi. Reconstructed by twentieth-
century scholars and archaeologists, Zhouyi presents the
highly imaginative world of myth and ritual that is the
hidden base of thousands of years of Eastern thought.

Now, for the first time ever, and after years of detailed
research and study, Stephen Karcher fuses these two
traditions using modern scholarship and archaeological
and linguistic research, along with a wide background
in Eastern philosophy and comparative religion, and
presents them to the modern Western reader in a
comprehensive, accessible and vivid new form.

Total I Ching is a complete oracle with instruction
for immediate use in all life situations. It is also the first
translation to detail the mythology of the divinatory
system, offering a revolutionary new approach to
the world's oldest wisdom tradition.

'This could be Karcher's masterpiece – a beautiful, liberating,
potent and inspiring version of the ancient classic . . . even
experienced users will be astonished by the extraordinary
riches they will find in *Total I Ching*'
Dr Roderick Main, Lecturer in Psychoanalytical Studies,
University of Essex

KUAN YIN

Stephen Karcher

Kuan Yin, the ancient Chinese goddess of Compassion, is the principal goddess in the Eastern firmament. Wherever there are Chinese- or Japanese-speaking people in the world – in homes, restaurants, workplaces, small urban temples and shrines – Kuan Yin's image can be found. The ritual of consulting her has brought solace, hope and insight to countless people and it continues to be an integral part of the lives of tens of millions of people throughout the East today.

Stephen Karcher's interpretation of this ancient text presents 'The 100 Poems of the Goddess', as relevant today as they were 1000 years ago, in an extremely easy to use and amazingly insightful form. Simply ask the oracle a question. By opening your heart to the answer, you allow yourself to be 're-arranged' by the symbol or figure Kuan Yin gives you. Then turn to the relevant page for that symbol in the book, where you will find directions to help you focus your energy and choose the right spiritual practice to find an answer.

Stephen Karcher Ph.D has worked with divinatory texts for more than thirty years. He is generally acknowledged to be one of the world's experts on the psychological and spiritual uses of divination and the relation of divination to the arts.

ESSENTIAL SHIATSU

Yuichi Kawada and Stephen Karcher

Shiatsu is a contemporary bodywork therapy that allows the mind and the body to work together harmoniously, helping to restore the great natural balance of the individual and the world. It is about making connections, connections to heaven that awaken and brighten us, helping us to reach health, happiness and peace, and connections to earth that let us fulfil the purpose of our lives.

The centre of Shiatsu is the sense of touch, offering a profound system of diagnosis and healing that seeks to help people by working with a person's natural forces – the meridian lines or energy channels whose malfunction can cause disorder and disease. In *Essential Shiatsu* Yuichi Kawada combines the preventative care of traditional shiatsu, with its twelve principal Meridians, with the crucial role of the Eight Extraordinary Meridians as rescue and emergency forces, while also drawing on traditional Eastern wisdom such as the *I Ching* and *The Yellow Emperor's Classic of Internal Medicine*.

Kawada's knowledge and understanding of the Eight Extraordinary Meridians is the outcome of a long period of experimentation, and here we see his mind and practice at work, offering a range of specific techniques and thoughts for both practitioner and layperson as aids to healthy and peaceful living.